CONTENTS

Contents

INTRODUCTION

What this book is about: ethics

Moral issues constantly make the headlines. For instance, there hasn't been a single day since the end of the Second World War when there hasn't been fighting somewhere in the world and, often, that fighting has involved British troops. This fact inevitably makes people ask questions such as 'Is this war worth fighting?' and 'Is any war worth fighting?'

Any answers we give are based on assumptions about what is right or wrong. Do we believe that it's right to use force? If so, when, and how much, force should be used? These assumptions might have come from a great deal of thinking or we might have picked them up from our families and friends.

When we ask questions about whether something is right or wrong, or good or evil, we are entering into a discussion about ethics (from the Ancient Greek word *ēthikos*, which is related to *ēthos*, meaning 'custom' or 'habit').

This book will help you to explore and understand a range of complicated ethical issues, such as:

- Should terminally ill people be helped to die?
- When is it justifiable to go to war?
- Should women with unwanted pregnancies have a right to abortion on demand?
- Should saving the environment be regarded as more important than anything else?

Each topic covers a major area and will help you not only to make up your own mind but also to understand a wide range of views, which will be important for your GCSE examinations.

Some of these topics will probably be quite familiar. However, the way people discuss them is often at the level of someone stopped in the street by a TV reporter. They are often a bit confused about what to say and find it difficult to give reasons for their opinions. Once you've read this book, and discussed and written about the topics, you should be able to express – and justify – your opinions clearly.

Keeping up to date

Every week there are changes – in the law or in medicine, for example – that might make the information in this book out of date. You should keep your knowledge of current affairs (the news) up to date. If you want to make sure you have the latest information, check on the Internet either by using searches or the website addresses given in each topic.

At the end, Topic 12 discusses the major approaches to ethics (ethical theory). You are likely to find this topic useful and interesting after you've studied the others, and it provides a link to A/S level.

The layout of each topic

The topics are laid out in a way that allows you to get to grips with them quickly.

- The **Personal stories** or **Stories** show that moral questions aren't theoretical: they affect real people.

- The **Discussion** helps you to see that each topic has a number of different angles.

- The **Glossary** defines technical terms.

- The **Introduction and main points** are provided once you've got a feel for the topic. The main points are those you have to know to form a justifiable opinion and to answer exam questions well.

- **Going deeper** gives you more information if a topic particularly interests you. It will also give you the material that coursework or assessment under controlled conditions will require.

- The **Summary** helps you with revision before exams. It lists essential information and ideas from the whole of each topic.

- The **Revision questions** help you to check that you've grasped the main points.

Attitudes towards animals

Should we eat them? Should we use them for medical experiments?

 Personal stories

Elaine took a job in a chicken processing factory before going to university. She was so disgusted by the experience of handling chicken carcasses day after day that she vowed never to eat meat again. Her friends are shocked at her decision as she had always liked Big Macs and fast food before this gap-year job. Elaine's mother is worried about whether she is getting a properly balanced diet. She also finds it a chore to have to cook special vegetarian meals for Elaine every day. Elaine's reply to her mum's complaints is: 'Why don't we all become vegetarian?' But none of the rest of her family is willing to give up meat.

A leading university has begun building a new medical research facility where scientists hope to develop new treatments for cancer. Some of the research will involve testing on small animals. Animal rights groups have found out about this and are organizing pickets which prevent contractors getting into the site to build the facility. Threatening letters have been sent to the scientists who will be working there. A counter-demonstration in favour of the new research facility has been organized.

Copyright © Press Association

Scientists researching Down's syndrome (which affects 1 in 8,000 births) have bred a mouse with Down's syndrome. They have done so to carry out genetic research into the condition. They have already identified the most important genes, but they have yet to develop and test drugs to prevent the disability. To do this, they need to test them on Down's syndrome mice and there are too few mice to do so. They want to breed more mice and need funding for this. They are wary of attracting publicity in case protesters target their work.

 Discussion

- Would you consider becoming a vegetarian?
- Would you protest against animal experiments?
- Would you defend the right of researchers to use animals for their research?

Glossary

speciesism favouring our species – and only according rights to human beings – at the expense of other species

vivisection literally means cutting up live animals and has come to refer to all experiments done with live animals

INTRODUCTION AND MAIN POINTS

Most people in the UK have little contact with farming or farm animals. The only animals that most of us encounter are pets or wild birds in parks and gardens, or in animal sanctuaries or zoos.

Food

But this does not prevent many of us from worrying about where our meat comes from and how it is raised. Supermarket labelling and advertising reflect this concern. Food is marketed as 'free from genetic modification'. Packaging tells us that meat comes from 'happy animals' that were raised in family groups and roamed free. Also, supermarkets have whole sections dedicated to 'organic' food and a growing number of people opt out of meat-eating entirely and become

vegetarian. Visit the Vegetarian Society's website www.vegsoc.org/statistics and find out how many vegetarians there are in the UK.

The use of animals in medical research

Many people are concerned about the use of animals in medical research. However, the UK Medical Research Council (MRC) insists that the use of animals in medical research is essential, although strict guidelines apply. When scientists apply for funds for studies involving animals, they must give sound scientific reasons to show that there is no alternative to using them.

The MRC operates according to the three Rs:

1 *replacement* of animals with humane alternatives whenever possible;

2 *reduction* in the number of animals used;

3 *refinement* of husbandry and procedures to minimize any pain and suffering the animals might experience and to improve animal welfare.

Animal rights

Taken together, concerns about where food comes from and how animals are raised and treated have given rise to a demand for 'animal rights'.

Some people feel so strongly about animal rights that they will not eat food that comes from animals. They are either vegetarians or vegans (who not only reject eating meat but will also not eat dairy products that come from animals). Others express their concern by protesting against medical experiments that entail the use of animals.

Animal welfare

At the heart of calls for 'animal rights' are concerns for 'animal welfare'.

> '**We believe that** an animal's welfare, whether on farm, in transit, at market or at a place of slaughter should be considered in terms of "five freedoms". These freedoms define ideal states rather than standards for acceptable welfare.'
>
> (Farm Animal Welfare Council website; www.fawc.org.uk/ freedoms.htm)

The Five Freedoms

Many people believe that animals, both pets and farm animals, should be looked after in a humane way. A popular way of expressing this is known as the Five Freedoms:

1 *Freedom from hunger and thirst* – through fresh water and a healthy diet.

2 *Freedom from discomfort* – through the right environment, including shelter and rest area.

3 *Freedom from pain, injury or disease* – through appropriate preventative measures and effective treatment.

4 *Freedom to express normal behaviour* – through adequate space, facilities and company of animals of the same kind.

5 *Freedom from fear and distress* – through conditions and treatment that avoid mental suffering.

Tesco supermarkets have adopted the Five Freedoms as a basis for the rearing of their organic meat range, calling them 'freedom foods'. It is a short step from claiming that animals *should* have certain freedoms to saying that human beings have a *duty* to provide the Five Freedoms and that animals have a *right* to the Five Freedoms.

But do animals have the same rights as humans?

Those who believe that animals have rights appear to be claiming that animals have rights like the ones that humans have, e.g. the right to life, freedom from suffering and freedom of movement.

Many people disagree with this approach because they believe that humans have rights partly because we are 'above' animals. (See 'Christian thinkers past and present' on page 14 for more about this issue.)

On the other hand, the fact that there are EU directives that oblige us to look after pets and farm animals in a particular way suggests that some sense of animal rights is becoming generally accepted.

Copyright © Shutterstock

Is it acceptable to carry out medical experiments on animals?

Many people are concerned about the use of animals for medical experiments (for a fuller discussion of this subject, see www.ypte.org. uk/environmental/vivisection/77).

The word **vivisection**, which literally means cutting up live animals, has come to refer to all experiments done with live animals.

The debate is between anti-vivisectionists who argue that vivisection is outdated and cruel to animals and often produces misleading results, and pro-vivisectionists who argue that medical advances partly depend on vivisection and that care is taken over the welfare of the animals used.

How many experiments are there?

Although there are fewer experiments carried out on animals today than in the 1980s, the number has remained fairly level since 2000. This trend is borne out by UK government statistics:

1987	3,631,400 procedures
2000	2,714,700 procedures
2001	2,622,400 procedures
2004	2,854,900 procedures.

Most procedures are carried out to research into the treatment of new diseases and for biological and medical research.

Which animals are used?

Some animals are bred with an inherited genetic defect for medical research. The vast majority of experiments are carried out on rats and mice and other rodents.

Very few (2 per cent) are carried out on large animals and less than 0.2 per cent on monkeys.

How much do the experiments cost? Who pays?

Most of the funding for the research comes directly or indirectly from industry (industry funds most university research), and 'industry' essentially means drug companies.

The development of new drugs is often enormously expensive. All laboratory testing

in the UK is regulated by law and supervised by government inspectors (but in 2005 there were only 20 or so inspectors).

What are the experiments for?

The experiments are primarily performed to expose risks that new medicines might have for human beings or to imitate diseases that we suffer from (e.g. cancer, cystic fibrosis or arthritis). Some promising research into Alzheimer's (memory loss disease) has involved the use of genetically modified mice. Cystic fibrosis has been accurately reproduced in genetically altered laboratory mice.

Is it acceptable to test cosmetics on animals?

The aspect of animal experimentation that has caused most public reaction has been that of using animals to test cosmetics. While it may be possible to justify the use of animals to test medicines or help people to recover from illnesses, cosmetic testing is harder to justify. Why, its opponents ask, should animals suffer to satisfy human vanity?

Testing cosmetics on animals is banned

For this reason, the UK government banned the use of animals for testing cosmetic products in 1998. However, opponents of the ban point out that this has had the effect of 'exporting' animal testing of cosmetics.

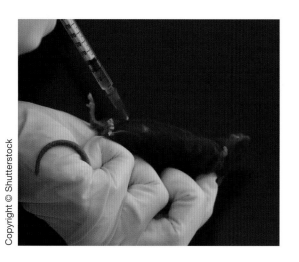

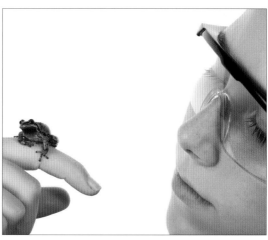

The late Dame Anita Roddick founded The Body Shop in 1976. Partly, she started the business to support her family but, she explained:

'It wasn't only economic necessity that inspired the birth of The Body Shop. My early travels had given me a wealth of experience. I had spent time in farming and fishing communities with pre-industrial peoples, and been exposed to body rituals of women from all over the world. Also the frugality that my mother exercised during the war years made me question retail conventions. Why waste a container when you can refill it? And why buy more of something than you can use? We behaved as she did in the Second World War, we reused everything, we refilled everything and we recycled all we could. The foundation of The Body Shop's environmental activism was born out of ideas like these.'

(www.anitaroddick.com/aboutanita.php)

Dame Anita Roddick showing the medal for services to retail, the environment and charity

The Body Shop

Anita Roddick founded The Body Shop with the express purpose of providing cosmetics that had not been tested on animals and that did not depend upon the exploitation of natural resources.

THE CHRISTIAN VIEW

Biblical ideas

Old Testament

In Genesis 1.28, the rest of creation is depicted as being 'beneath' human beings and under their control: 'God blessed them, and God said to them, "Be fruitful and multiply, and fill the earth and *subdue* it; and *have dominion* over the fish of the sea and over the birds of the air and over every living thing that moves upon the earth".' This text raises the question of whether human beings can simply do what they like with animals.

In the next chapter of Genesis, human beings are also likened to a gardener: 'The LORD God took the man and put him in the garden of Eden *to till it and keep it*' (Genesis 2.15). But human beings are still at the centre of the story. We are given the power to name every living creature, which suggests that we are 'above' that which cannot name itself: 'whatever the man called each living creature, that was its name' (Genesis 2.19).

It is not until Genesis 9 that human beings are given clear permission to eat meat. This describes the time when Noah's flood is over and God tells him and his family that they may eat 'every moving thing that lives' (Genesis 9.3).

In Leviticus 14 and Deuteronomy 14, lists are provided of animals that are 'clean' or 'unclean' and that may or may not be eaten.

So, although it appears that mankind was vegetarian before the flood, humanity was later allowed by God to eat meat. Christians, therefore, have been content to eat meat. (For comment about this, see 'Christian thinkers past and present', page 14.)

God's care for animals is shown in Psalm 36.6: 'you save humans and animals alike, O LORD'. And people are expected to care for them, too: 'A good man takes care of his animals, but wicked men are cruel to theirs' (Proverbs 12.10, GNB).

New Testament

We often raise moral questions today that could not have occurred to people at the time of Jesus. For example: should we eat genetically modified foods? Are nuclear weapons permissible? 'Would Jesus want us to eat meat?' is a question such as this. There is no record of his having taught about this, nor are there many references to his eating. We can say that he ate fish but that does not mean all Christians should or should not eat fish.

However, some Christians latch on to the fact that Jesus spoke kindly about animals, that he lived among wild animals in the wilderness, and that St Luke implies that Jesus was born among farm animals.

More generally, some Christians will point out that Jesus was on the side of the weak and the oppressed and class animals today as belonging to the 'weak and oppressed'.

New Testament passages that illustrate God's attitude towards animals include Matthew 6.26: 'Look at the birds of the air . . . your heavenly Father feeds them.'

 GOING DEEPER

Christian thinkers past and present

There is a wide variety of Christian thought about how humans should regard animals. On the one hand, Christian thinkers like St Thomas Aquinas and Karl Barth view man as simply superior to animals. At the other extreme, thinkers like Peter Singer assert that the fact that animals can suffer makes them very close to human beings.

If you find yourself in agreement with Aquinas or Barth, you are more likely to find animal experiments for medical research acceptable than if your views are close to Peter Singer's.

Humans' superiority to the rest of creation	**St Thomas Aquinas** (*c.* 1225–1274) Aquinas was one of the most influential Christian thinkers. His ideas owed a great deal to the thought of the Greek philosopher Aristotle. Aquinas regarded animals and plants as inferior to human beings because they could not reason and had no soul. They were created simply for the use of humans and had no rights. This view probably remains the most widely held Christian attitude to animals. **Karl Barth** (1886–1968) Karl Barth was a Swiss theologian who had as great an influence on twentieth-century Christian thinking as Albert Einstein had on physics. Almost recalling Aquinas' approach, Barth argued that since God became a human being in Jesus Christ, that made *human* nature superior to all other life forms. Copyright © Press Association
Animals suffering establishes common ground between animals and humans	**Albert Schweitzer** (1875–1965) Schweitzer was famous as a theologian, musician, doctor and missionary. He received the Nobel Prize for his philosophy of reverence for life. He believed that human beings have a will to live and are surrounded by other creatures with a will to live. However, we differ from other creatures in being aware of this 'will to live' in all creatures, which should lead us to treat our own life and that of other creatures with equal reverence. We also have the moral responsibility only Copyright © Press Association

	to take life when necessary, which means that Schweitzer's philosophy would sanction farming animals for food and using them for medical experiments, but would forbid hunting animals for sport. Schweitzer illustrated his philosophy with this little story: 'Beyond the unavoidable, I must never go, not even with what seems insignificant. The farmer, who has mown down a thousand flowers in his meadow as fodder for his cows, must be careful on his way home not to strike off in wanton pastime the head of a single flower by the roadside, for he thereby commits a wrong against life without being under the pressure of necessity' (from *The Philosophy of Civilization*).
In an ideal world (and human beings have spoiled the world) meat eating would be unnecessary	**Andrew Linzey** (1952–)  Copyright © Andrew Linzey Andrew Linzey, a leading thinker about animal ethics, argues that Christians should be vegetarians. He bases his argument on the description of human beings in Genesis. Humans are given rule over the creatures of the earth (Genesis 1.26) and plants bear seeds and fruit to eat, i.e. a vegetarian diet (Genesis 1.29). There is no mention of humans eating animals. Only later in Genesis is Noah told that he and his family can eat everything that moves (Genesis 9.3). And this meat eating comes with conditions: 'you shall not eat flesh with its life, that is, its blood. *For I shall require an account of all blood shed*, from beast and man' (Genesis 9.4–5; Linzey's own translation). Linzey interprets this as meaning that human beings will have to justify to God any killing of animals. This means, Linzey believes, that animal life can only be taken in exceptional circumstances and for good reason.
Campaigning for the rights of animals is comparable to earlier campaigning for racial equality and for gender equality	**Peter Singer** (1946–) Peter Singer is an Australian philosopher well known for his work on animal ethics. Singer compares the campaign for the rights of animals to the earlier campaigns for racial and gender equality. He is aware that this claim may appear laughable because animals are so obviously different from humans. But he argues that racial and gender equality don't depend on men and women or different races being *identical*, but upon their having the *same* physical characteristics. Singer believes that 'similar characteristics' – particularly awareness, including the capacity for suffering – mean that there is no dividing line between human beings and animals. This means that animals have rights as well as humans. To restrict rights to human beings is to be prejudiced in favour of our species: **speciesism**.

⊚ SUMMARY

1 Most people have little contact with animals, apart from pets or wild birds.

2 Anxiety occurs about the origins of food; hence a market for 'organic' food and fear of genetically modified products.

3 There is widespread concern for animal welfare and opposition to animals being used in scientific research.

4 The *Five Freedoms* are used as an approach to animal welfare. They are freedom from hunger and thirst; discomfort; pain, injury and disease; from restrictions on normal behaviour; and fear and distress.

5 It is a short step from claiming that animals *should* have certain freedoms to saying that human beings have a *duty* to provide them.

6   The use of animals in experiments (vivisection) causes controversy. Vivisection means 'cutting up live animals' but in practice refers to all animal experiments.

7   The number of animal experiments is in decline and most are on rats, mice and other rodents.

8   The Bible offers conflicting guidance. Genesis 1.28 appears to give humans *dominion* over the rest of creation, which is *beneath* us. Genesis 2 portrays humans as gardeners who have stewardship of a creation which is *beneath* us. But clear permission to eat meat only comes in Genesis 9 when Noah's flood occurs (they may eat 'everything that moves').

9   There is nothing in the New Testament about whether eating meat is permissible (but nor is there about nuclear weapons, etc.). It was not a question that arose for Jesus and his contemporaries. However, some people argue that Jesus was on the side of the weak and oppressed, so he would be on the side of defenceless animals, but most Christians would not agree with this argument.

10   The prevalent attitude among Christians might change in time as the number of vegetarians has increased recently (doubling to 5 per cent of the adult population in the last 10 years).

11   A range of Christian thinkers can be broadly divided into two groups: those who see animals as inferior to humans (and this view has dominated Christian thought until recently) and those who are concerned for the proper treatment of animals and their rights.

GOING DEEPER

12   St Thomas Aquinas regarded animals as inferior to humans, the prevailing modern view. Karl Barth believed that since God became human in Christ, human nature was superior.

13   Albert Schweitzer believed in the sanctity of all creation and that we should have a 'reverence for life'.

14   Andrew Linzey (b. 1952), the author of *Why Animal Suffering Matters: Philosophy, theology and practical ethics* and *Creatures of the Same God: Explorations in animal theology*, argues that God gave conditional permission to humans to eat meat. Ideally, we should not eat meat.

15   Peter Singer claims that animals have rights like humans. Restricting rights to humans is to favour our species at the expense of other species – speciesism. Singer argues that the shared capacity for suffering gives *both* humans and animals rights.

✓ REVISION QUESTIONS

1 Name a common anxiety about food.

2 List the Five Freedoms.

3 Why may concerns about animal welfare lead to a call for animal rights?

4 What is the general term for experiments on animals?

5 Why are some people in favour of the use of animals in experiments?

6 Why are some people opposed to the use of animals in experiments?

7 Which animals are most commonly experimented upon?

8 Which particular kind of experimentation upon animals is not permitted in the UK?

9 What are the principal ideas about the relationship between humans and animals that can be found in Genesis 1?

10 What is the significance of the passage in Genesis 9 for ethics about food?

11 How might it be possible to argue that Jesus would have supported animal rights?

GOING DEEPER

12 Summarize Andrew Linzey's argument about meat eating.

13 Why does Peter Singer accord animals rights?

14 What is meant by speciesism?

Assisted conception

Personal stories

Jean and her partner, Rob, are both carriers of cystic fibrosis (CF), the most common genetic disease. If Jean becomes pregnant naturally, there is a 25 per cent chance that the child will have CF and a 50 per cent chance that the child will be a carrier.

Some of Jean's family members have died of CF (the average life expectancy is 37) and she is not prepared to risk a child of hers having to live with CF and die young. The only certain way to have a baby without CF is to conceive using *in vitro* fertilization (**IVF**), to have a 'test-tube baby'.

Cystic fibrosis is an inherited (genetic) disease. To develop the condition, you need to inherit two cystic fibrosis genes, one from each parent. If you inherit only one gene, you are a carrier and have no symptoms.

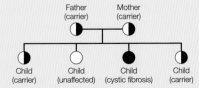

If both parents are carriers, the odds are:
- a 1 in 4 chance of having a child with cystic fibrosis;
- a 1 in 2 chance of having a child who is a carrier;
- a 1 in 4 chance of having an unaffected child.

Rosita's husband Raoul died after suffering a very severe head injury in a car accident. Before he died, he was in a coma (he didn't regain consciousness) for several days. Before the accident Raoul and Rosita had been trying for a baby. Up to this time, they had not been successful. Even though Rosita is confronted with the certainty of Raoul's death, she wants to find some way of having his baby.

Rosita has read that doctors can collect **sperm** from unconscious patients so she asks them to carry out this procedure on him. They are sympathetic but unable to do anything unless she can prove that this would have been his wish.

Adding sperm to eggs in the laboratory

Jared has been married for some time and has two children. His sister is also married but she was only able to start a family through using **artificial insemination by donor (AID)**.

Because Jared has seen the benefits of AID in his own family, he would like to help other couples conceive through making a donation of his sperm. However, a new development in the law is making him hesitate. The new law permits children born from donated sperm to discover the identity of their genetic fathers once they have reached the age of 18. He is not sure how he would cope with genetic children of his, whom he had never previously met, trying to make contact with him once they were young adults.

(*The Times*, 22 November 2005)

Glossary

artificial insemination by donor (AID) an anonymous donation of healthy sperm from another man is implanted into a woman's uterus

artificial insemination by husband (AIH) sperm is taken from a man and implanted into his partner's uterus

blastocyst a hollow ball of cells and inner cell mass that represents an early stage of embryonic development

blastomere a cell produced by the division of a fertilized egg

embryo in humans, the name given to the developing organism between fertilization and the end of the eighth week of development (gestation)

encyclical an authoritative letter sent by the Pope to all the other bishops in the Roman Catholic Church to assist them in their teaching of the faith to all Catholics

eugenic having the intention of producing good or improved offspring

fertilization happens when a sperm successfully penetrates an ovum and cell division starts

foetus in humans, the name given to the developing organism after the embryonic stage and before birth

in vitro **fertilization (IVF)** fertilizing a woman's egg (ovum) with a man's sperm *in vitro* ('in glass', actually in a Petri dish). The fertilized ovum is returned to the woman's uterus

insemination introduction of sperm into the female uterus (womb) during copulation (sex); it may occur artificially – hence artificial insemination (e.g. IVF, AIH, AID – all explained in this topic)

morula a solid ball of cells, the intermediate stage between first fertilization of the ovum and the blastocyst

ovum from the Latin word of the same spelling, meaning an egg – refers to the female reproductive cell (plural ova)

preimplantation genetic diagnosis (PGD) a procedure for determining whether an embryo is carrying a genetic disease

sanctity of life life is of special value because it is the gift of God (the word sanctity is related to the Latin word for holy, *sanctus*, which is one of the qualities of God)

sperm from Greek *sperma* meaning 'seed' – refers to the male reproductive cells

zygote first cell formed when a new organism is produced through the means of sexual reproduction (a fertilized, undivided egg)

Discussion

- Do you think that children should be brought into being through IVF?
- Who should be given IVF?
- Would you feel happy about children who owed their lives to your donation of genetic material (sperm or ova) finding out your identity as their genetic parent? Bear in mind that this might happen 18 years or so after you gave genetic material.

INTRODUCTION AND MAIN POINTS

Most people want to have children but a significant minority (about 10 per cent) cannot conceive naturally. However, since 1978, when the first IVF baby was born, medical assistance has helped couples overcome their infertility.

Techniques

Today, there are three principal techniques of assisted conception available: **artificial insemination by husband (AIH)**, artificial

Louise Brown, aged 10, the world's first test-tube baby

insemination by donor (AID) and *in vitro* fertilization (IVF).

Artificial insemination by husband (AIH)

AIH is used when tests show that a man's sperm are healthy but his partner is either not releasing an egg for **fertilization** or his sperm cannot reach the egg to fertilize it. To remedy this, sperm is taken from the man and implanted in the woman's uterus.

Religious viewpoint

Those who favour this technique argue that, through advances in science, human beings are using their God-given intelligence and ability to reason in order to help a couple to have a child. Also, although some medical intervention is necessary, the parents of any children that are born from this method are the genetic parents of the child. However, Roman Catholics argue that this interference is unnatural and so against the will of God. They might also argue that the infertility of some couples helps to keep the overall population down, which benefits the rest of humanity in an 'overcrowded world' (but artificial contraception, to which Roman Catholics also object, is the greatest cause of population limitation).

Artificial insemination by donor (AID)

AID is used when the woman is fertile but her partner is not. The principal reason for such infertility in men is that they produce insufficient sperm to fertilize a woman's eggs. To remedy this problem, an anonymous donation of healthy sperm from another man can be implanted in the woman's uterus.

Religious viewpoint

Although AID entails only the mother having a genetic relationship to the baby, many couples prefer this to having no children. The Church of England accepts AID, although not where sperm donation has been the result of

payment to a donor. The Church of England also insists that proper records are kept to enable children to identify their genetic father when they become adults, if they wish. The Roman Catholic Church argues that AID amounts to adultery because, just as in adultery, the child has been conceived through the **insemination** of a woman with sperm other than her partner's (however, it is not the same as adultery, as there is no question of another intimate relationship).

In vitro fertilization (IVF)

IVF involves fertilizing a woman's egg (**ovum**) with a man's sperm *in vitro*. The fertilized ovum is then returned to the woman's uterus.

Copyright © Shutterstock

Freezing embryos for storage

'**Over the [past] few years**, we have developed a successful intracytoplasmic sperm injection (ICSI) . . . This procedure is used to treat severe male factor infertility. It opens the door to a large number of men who would otherwise be considered totally sterile. With this ICSI procedure, each egg is injected with a single sperm, one at a time. Therefore, only a few sperm are needed. In some effectively sterile men, the sperm need to be obtained surgically. We now are able to carry out this procedure under light anesthesia right in the office, with the help of several urologists. The sperm can be taken by aspirating the testicle itself or the surrounding tubules. Excess sperm can be frozen for future use. Since this process will help a very significant number of infertile couples, it is probably one of the most significant advances in IVF since the very beginning.'

(Website of The Women's Clinic, PA; http://infertilitypa.com/ivf.htm)

Embryo research

The introduction of IVF has also made possible research on human **embryos**. Embryo research has enabled scientists to treat and detect hereditary diseases and genetic defects, and the causes of poor fertility and infertility.

However, such research has raised many ethical questions. Primarily, if you take the Christian view that life is sacred, you may object to any such research. Whether you do depends upon how you regard the embryo. For many Roman Catholics, life begins at conception, so embryo research might mean the misuse of a human life or a potential human life and should not be permitted (see the

Catechism of the Catholic Church, paras 2270 and 2273). Fertilizing an egg and destroying it after 14 days (which the Human Fertilisation and Embryology Authority (HFEA) requires) amounts to 'taking a life' and breaking the Sixth Commandment. Anglicans take a slightly different view. The Church of England's response to embryo research is: 'We support the recommendation that research, under licence, be permitted on embryos up to 14 days old and agree that embryos should not be created purely for scientific research'. This means that Anglicans believe that embryo research is possible under strict controls.

Religious viewpoint

When IVF involves the use of an ovum from one member of a couple and sperm from the other, you could argue that the end product, a fertilized ovum, is identical with that which occurs through the means of normal sexual intercourse. However, Roman Catholics disagree with the way in which IVF separates procreation (making the child) from sexual relations within the loving context of a marriage. In this way, there is no immediate connection between conception and the sexual act ('they separate procreation from the fully human context of the conjugal act' – Pope John Paul II), they are not the direct consequence of an act of love.

But some people see IVF as simply a technique (possibly one requiring some practical safeguards) that gives couples who might otherwise not have a baby the chance to have one. You might even regard the medical process as something done to help conception within the context of a marriage or lasting partnership.

A Church of England briefing paper bases this view on the following argument:

> The reason some find embryo testing and disposal acceptable is that for the first 14 days of an embryo's life, if it were created in the ordinary way, it would not have settled in the wall of the mother's womb, but would be

making its way there. During this time the embryo might be washed out, or it might divide and become identical twins, or even triplets. The Warnock Commission, which gave rise to the Human Fertilisation and Embryology Act 1990, took this view, that for 14 days the embryo could be treated as a non-person, though with respect for the person it could become.

Many Christians believe that scientific skills are a gift from God and experiments can be used to relieve suffering and demonstrate love for their neighbours.

Cloning

Cloning means making an identical copy of something. In a medical context, cloning is done for its health benefits. There are three main types: embryo cloning, reproductive cloning and therapeutic cloning.

Embryo cloning

This imitates the natural process whereby twins or triplets are produced – it can be described as 'artificial twinning'. One or more cells are removed from a fertilized embryo in the hope that they will develop into duplicate embryos. This technique has been employed with animals for a long time but experimentation on humans has been very limited.

Reproductive cloning technique applied to animals

Scientists take a normal cell from an animal's body intending to convert it into an embryo. To do this, they remove an egg from the animal they want to clone. Next, they remove the nucleus – which contains the animal's DNA – from the egg, which leaves an empty egg containing no DNA. They then take a cell from elsewhere in that or another animal's body (e.g. its skin or udder), remove its nucleus and insert it into the empty egg cell. The two are fused through the use of an electric shock. The empty egg cell provides a good environment in which the donor animal's genetic information (DNA) can dictate normal development (cell division into two, four, eight cells, etc.).

This may sound like a simple process but in fact it is fraught with complications. It took researchers at the Roslin Institute 276 attempts before the cloned sheep Dolly was born.

To prove that the ewe that gave birth to Dolly had not been made pregnant accidentally, they chose an all-white sheep – a Finn Dorset – for the donor nucleus; the ewe that gave birth to Dolly was a Blackface and this breed always passes on this unique characteristic. Since Dolly was all white, she could not have been the genetic lamb of the ewe that gave birth to her.

Dolly the sheep: the first mammal to be cloned from an adult cell

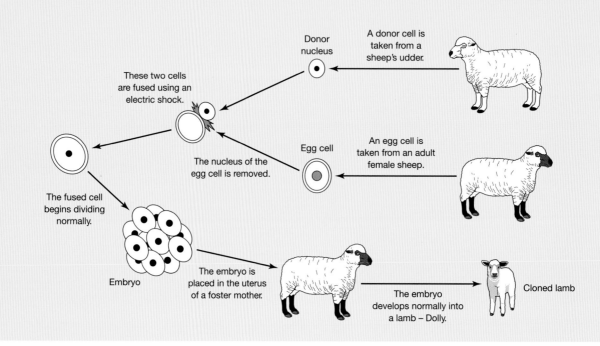

Donor nucleus

A donor cell is taken from a sheep's udder.

These two cells are fused using an electric shock.

The nucleus of the egg cell is removed.

Egg cell

An egg cell is taken from an adult female sheep.

The fused cell begins dividing normally.

Embryo

The embryo is placed in the uterus of a foster mother.

The embryo develops normally into a lamb – Dolly.

Cloned lamb

Reproductive cloning

Reproductive cloning aims to produce a duplicate of an animal. 'Dolly the sheep' reared at the Roslin Institute is the most famous example. DNA from an adult animal is placed in an embryo which has been enucleated (its nucleus has been removed). The embryo is then implanted in the womb of a ewe and allowed to develop into a lamb. As far as is known, this technique has never been attempted on humans and to attempt human reproductive cloning is illegal in the UK and many other countries.

Why would someone want to clone a human being?

There are several reasons why someone might want to clone a human being. For example, to:

1 create a child who can donate tissue to a sibling;
2 replace a child lost through accident or disease;
3 create a copy of a very gifted person (sportsman, musician, scientist, etc.);
4 give homosexual couples children related to one of the partners;
5 help with fertility problems;
6 make the pioneer researcher famous.

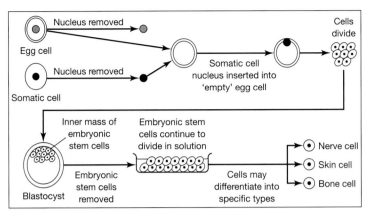

The therapeutic cloning process

Therapeutic cloning

Therapeutic cloning – also known as somatic cell nuclear transfer (SCNT) – first involves scientists removing the nucleus from an egg. They then extract the nucleus from a somatic cell (any body cell other than an egg or sperm) removed from the patient requiring treatment and substitute it for the nucleus removed from the egg.

The egg now contains the patient's genetic material. Once this has happened, the egg is stimulated to produce a cell cluster (**blastocyst**), with an outer and inner layer of cells. The inner cell mass, rich in stem cells, is isolated and these are used to produce embryonic stem cell lines. These cells are 'pluripotent', which means that they can give rise to any type of body cell apart from an embryo. Potentially, they could be used to treat diseases or replace damaged or dysfunctional cells. Also, since they contain the patient's genetic code, they will not be rejected in the way that cells transplanted from another person are. The embryo dies in the process.

Embryo cloning: issues raised by cloning techniques

Using animals

At present many people die because there is a shortage of human organs for transplant. Scientists are trying to create transgenic pigs with human genes so that a supply of hearts, livers and kidneys would be available for transplant into humans. Cloning these pigs would make it possible to provide as many organs as needed for transplant.

Those who believe in animal rights would argue that we should not 'make' animals simply for our own benefit. Note the summary of basic beliefs from the Oxford Centre for Animal Ethics, particularly the final two points which assert that we should not treat animals as 'resources' and that they 'should be treated with respect'.

Cloning and the law

There is broad international agreement to ban reproductive human cloning. In the UK, the Reproductive Cloning Act 2001 prohibited reproductive cloning. In 2005, a non-binding United Nations Declaration on Human Cloning called for all forms of human cloning contrary to human dignity to be banned and the Charter of Fundamental Rights of the European Union prohibits reproductive human cloning.

However, the law about therapeutic cloning in different countries is subject to change and development. For example, therapeutic cloning is permitted in some Australian states and, in the USA in 2009, President Obama reversed his predecessor's ban on government funding and support for therapeutic cloning. The UK has also seen considerable changes since 2001. The Human Fertilisation and Embryology (Research Purposes) Regulations 2001 amended the Human Fertilisation and Embryology Act (HFEA) 1990, to permit therapeutic cloning, and the HFEA 2008 permitted experiments on hybrid human–animal embryos.

The summary of animal ethics

'Animal ethics:

- is inspired by the work of ethicists and philosophers who have pioneered new perspectives on animals;
- is informed by scientific work indicating that animals are sentient and possess complex systems of awareness;
- seeks to relate these insights to how we treat animals today;
- questions the "old view" of animals as simply things, machines, tools, commodities, or resources, put here for our use, and
- holds that all sentient beings have intrinsic value and should be treated with respect.'

(www.oxfordanimalethics.com/about-the-centre/animal-ethics/)

Benefits for humans

Cloning of human embryos might assist in the understanding of what causes miscarriages. Eventually, such knowledge might help women who cannot carry a baby to full term to be able to do so successfully.

It might also advance understanding of how the **morula** (mass of cells that has developed from a blastocyst) attaches itself to the wall of the uterus. This might enable better, safer contraceptives to be developed. The rapid growth of the human morula resembles that of cancer cells. Researchers believe that finding a way to stop the division of the human ovum might lead to techniques for stopping the growth of cancers.

Parents who are at risk of passing on a genetic defect could make use of cloning. A fertilized ovum could be cloned and the clone could be tested to see whether it had the disorder. If it did not, the surviving clone could be allowed to develop into a baby.

In IVF, doctors begin by taking several ova, fertilize them with sperm and implant them in the woman's womb, hoping that one will result in a successful pregnancy. However, some women can only produce a single egg. Embryo cloning would give such women a better chance of getting pregnant – several ova rather than one would be available for implanting.

Cloning might also help to produce a 'spare parts bank'. An ovum might be fertilized and then cloned into multiple fertilized ova. One would be implanted in a woman and lead to the birth of a normal baby. The other fertilized eggs (**zygotes**) could be frozen and then – possibly in the remote future – one of them could be allowed to mature into a baby to provide, for instance, a bone marrow transplant for its twin.

Cloning could be used artificially to produce identical twins for these reasons:

- to minimize career disruption (the mother wishing to take maternity leave only once, whereas if she had two separate children she would require maternity leave on two occasions);
- to make a normal delivery possible (twin **foetuses** are smaller);
- to prevent the discomfort of a second pregnancy;
- to have children who could donate organs to a sibling.

Religious viewpoint

There are two principal Christian objections to the issues raised by cloning techniques.

1 Embryos could be injured or killed in any of these procedures, so the '**sanctity of life**' arguments apply. Those who are pro-life argue that the embryo is a person and – through the cloning procedures – at risk of assault or murder. The procedures treat the embryo not as a person but as a 'thing', a commodity.

2 There is the possibility – admittedly belonging to the sci-fi genre – of a country trying to produce an unlimited number of clones either in a **eugenic** way, to produce 'super humans' or to produce a slave class, which would be of low intelligence. Either of these possibilities could involve treating the persons that resulted as objects to be 'manufactured' rather than as fully unique persons.

Objections to reproductive cloning

There are several basic reasons why reproductive cloning is banned in the UK and many other countries.

A means to an end

Reproductive cloning differs from IVF. In IVF, the end result is to produce a child valuable in itself whom a couple could not otherwise conceive. It could be argued that a reproductive clone baby would be produced not because it is valuable in itself as a child but because someone wanted to replicate another human being. Reproductive cloning, therefore, treats the clone as a means to an end, not as an end in itself. This undermines the human dignity of the cloned human being.

Moreover, the woman providing the ova would have to give many more than just those needed for IVF, and so would be treated more as a 'natural resource' than as a person.

Unacceptable medical risks

Reproductive cloning entails many efforts that end in failure (it took 276 attempts before Dolly the sheep was born) and clones often have fatal or serious illness, which means that they do not survive long. To create human beings, each with the prospect of poor health and a short life, would not respect their rights – they would have been created as the means to an end of satisfying someone else's desires.

Psychological harm

It is arguable that producing a twin to replace a dead child or to complete a family might mean that children born later have to cope with not being valued in themselves.

Respect for human dignity

There is a remote possibility that human beings might be manufactured to produce either superior or inferior people, robbing them of their human dignity, treating the clones as a means to an end, not an end in themselves.

Therapeutic cloning: issues raised by cloning techniques

In 2001, the UK became the first country in the world to permit therapeutic cloning, and the Human Fertilisation and Embryology Act was amended to reflect this fact. The Human Reproductive Cloning Act was also passed in the same year. However, the government legislated at the same time to prohibit reproductive cloning.

In 2004, the first licence was granted to researchers at Newcastle University to investigate treatments for diabetes, Parkinson's disease and Alzheimer's. All research has to be licensed by the Human Fertilisation and Embryology Authority (HFEA).

Religious viewpoint

Some Christians welcome this research as a good stewardship of human beings' God-given intellectual and technological ability. They point to the great potential benefits to humanity because the research could result in cures for serious illnesses.

However, others are opposed, arguing that it is a fundamental Christian principle that the ends (the relief of human suffering caused by disease) cannot justify the means (the production of human embryos – which they regard as fully human – only to be discarded). Every human life, at every stage from conception to death, deserves respect (the sanctity-of-life argument).

They also argue that there is a 'slippery slope' from therapeutic cloning to reproductive cloning. Once cloned embryos are created, it is only necessary to implant them in someone's womb for reproductive cloning to happen. They also argue that it would be very difficult to regulate such actions.

Stem-cell research: issues raised by cloning techniques

Principal ethical objections to stem-cell research focus on the fact that it entails the destruction of an embryo. If you believe that life begins as soon as an embryo exists (which occurs once a sperm has fertilized an ovum), you will regard this procedure as involving abortion. It is seen as destroying one life to save or improve another. The debate about this has been particularly intense in the USA, where the 'Religious Right' has been vigorously opposed to stem-cell research, even though many people support it in the hope that incurable diseases can be cured.

Some argue that the whole process is unnecessary as adult stem cells can be used for therapies. However, adult stem cells do not differentiate into as many types of cell as embryonic stem cells do.

Supporters of embryonic stem-cell research, however, do not regard the embryo at this stage as a human life and they point to the great benefits to individuals and society in curing disease – suffering is ended and large sums of money that would be spent on sustaining sick people are saved.

Another argument often made in favour of therapeutic cloning is that it makes good use of the surplus embryos produced in IVF treatment (you only implant one or two from those fertilized). They would otherwise be discarded. The same argument may be applied to using embryos from legal abortions. However, this argument is rejected by those who are opposed to IVF treatment and legal abortions, on the grounds that human life is being taken (we return to sanctity-of-life arguments).

Copyright © Sophie Dean 2010; www.bitbookish.com

Possible alternatives to stem cells from embryos

1 Obtaining embryonic stem cells without destroying the embryo. Theoretically, lines of stem cells could be obtained from **blastomeres** without harming the embryo. Embryos that have had blastomeres extracted for **preimplantation genetic diagnosis (PGD)** have developed into normal children. However, it is not known whether there are any long-term side effects. Also, it is unclear whether stem-cell lines can be obtained from just a few blastomeres.

2 Obtaining embryonic stem cells without creating an embryo. Certain genes are removed from the nucleus of a somatic cell before it is inserted into an egg cell to prevent it from becoming a human embryo. It would simply be a 'biological artefact'. Once the stem cells are extracted from this biological artefact, the genes that were removed before the somatic cell nucleus was inserted into the egg cell would be reinserted. This procedure results in pluripotent stem cells.

 GOING DEEPER

Contrasted approaches to IVF among the main Christian Churches

Roman Catholic Church
The most recent and influential summary of Roman Catholic teaching about artificially assisted reproduction is given in *Evangelium Vitae*, an **encyclical** (the term means 'going the rounds of the earth'). This was published by Pope John Paul II (1920–2005; pope 1978–2005).

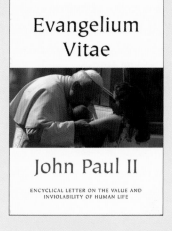

'**The various techniques of artificial reproduction**, which would seem to be at the service of life and which are frequently used with this intention, actually open the door to new threats against life. Apart from the fact that they are morally unacceptable, since they separate procreation from the fully human context of the conjugal act, these techniques have a high rate of failure: not just failure in relation to fertilization but with regard to the subsequent development of the embryo, which is exposed to the risk of death, generally within a very short space of time. Furthermore, the number of embryos produced is often greater than that needed for implantation in the woman's womb, and these so-called "spare embryos" are then destroyed or used for research which, under the pretext of scientific or medical progress, in fact reduces human life to the level of simple "biological material" to be freely disposed of.'

(John Paul II, *Evangelium Vitae*, section 14)

He lists objections to artificial techniques of reproduction. They:

- 'open the door to new threats against life';
- set apart the act of reproduction from making love/having sex ('separate procreation from the fully human context of the conjugal act');
- often don't succeed;
- produce embryos that often only live for a short time;
- produce 'spare embryos' that will either be destroyed or used for research in such a way that human life is reduced to the 'level of "simple biological material" to be freely disposed of'.

Church of England
The Church of England believes that using donations of sperm and eggs is an acceptable way to help a couple fulfil their desire to have a child. Anglicans add that the children conceived in this manner should have access to information concerning the donor. See the section on AID on page 20.

The Church of England has a different stance from the Catholics on the status of the embryo. Lord Habgood, a former Anglican Archbishop of York, said concerning embryos: 'At this earliest stage of their existence, embryos do not have the moral value of persons. They are to be treated with respect, but essentially they are no different from the product of early miscarriages.'

The Church of England therefore teaches that it is fine to create spare embryos which are later destroyed or not needed. They also believe that it is acceptable to carry out research on embryos for up to 14 days.

For the Church of England, IVF, AID and AIH are all acceptable methods of creating new life.

The Rt Revd Lord Habgood, a former Archbishop of York, seen here with the naturalist and broadcaster David Attenborough

How the provision of IVF is regulated in the UK and some of the principal issues

Human Fertilisation and Embryology Act (HFEA)
There is a wide variety of attitudes to IVF and other forms of fertility treatment. But in the United Kingdom, an Act of Parliament, the Human Fertilisation and Embryology Act 1990 (HFEA 1990) prescribes what treatment is permissible. Since 1990, there have been revisions to accommodate developments in reproductive technology.

The practical enforcement of the Act's provisions is regulated by the Human Fertilisation and Embryology Authority (also HFEA). The Act requires clinics offering assisted conception to consider the welfare of any child born as a result of treatment and the welfare of any existing child of the family before they agree to provide treatment.

The HFEA provides clinics with guidelines to help them to act legally in accordance with the Act. These guidelines presume that treatment should be offered unless there is evidence that the child is 'likely to experience serious harm'. This enables most patients to receive treatment 'with the minimum of delay'. But it also means that treatment is not offered in a small minority of cases. See the HFEA website for fuller explanation of the process of applying for IVF treatment (www.hfea.gov.uk).

Why do people donate sperm, eggs or embryos?

Donors are often people who have been able to have children themselves and who want to help others who are unable to conceive naturally. Those others might include friends or members of their families.

If individuals decide to become donors, their decision has a big effect on the children that might result (they wouldn't exist otherwise) and on their families if they have them (because their own children would have unknown siblings or half-siblings). Donating genetic material is not like donating blood: new human beings might result from a gift.

Sperm, egg and embryo donors are no longer anonymous

Men donating sperm between 1991 and 1 April 2005 could do so and remain anonymous. They were simply asked for some 'non-identifying information' which could be given to people choosing a donor for treatment, and to people conceived from donations (when they reach the age of 18).

The law was changed to take account of 'how important it would be for some donor-conceived people to find out more about

their genetic origins'. Consequently, people born as a result of donated sperm, eggs or embryos may ask the HFEA for identifying information once they reach the age of 18.

Finding out about children born from a donation

The HFEA has to keep a record of 'all assisted reproduction treatments, including those using donated sperm, eggs or embryos, and the outcome of those treatments. This record is known as the HFEA Register' (www.hfea.gov.uk/infertility-facts.html).

A donor is entitled to know if a child was born as a result of a donation, what the child's gender is and the year of his or her birth. Only ten families can be created from a donation. Children born from donations will also be able to contact the HFEA when they reach the age of 18 and ask for information about their genetic parents.

Can IVF be performed even if the sperm donor is dead?

In 1997, there was a famous legal case involving Diane Blood. She and her husband had hoped to have children but he died before she was able to conceive. However, she had sperm removed from his body and stored in the hope that she would be able to conceive after his death (posthumously).

There was considerable public sympathy for Mrs Blood's desire to have a baby even though her husband had died. After all, many people argued, women sometimes (particularly, for example, in war time) gave birth to children after their husbands had died.

A complex legal process ensued. The High Court upheld the HFEA's rejection of Mrs Blood's request to have a baby by artificial insemination with her dead husband's sperm. The rejection was based on the 1990 Human Fertilisation and Embryology Act, which banned the taking of sperm without written consent. However, Mrs Blood took her case to the Court of Appeal (the next level of court after the High Court), which ruled that Mrs Blood's case was unique. It was judged that the HFEA should have exercised its discretion

Diane Blood with her two sons, who were conceived after their father's death

should be allowed to seek fertility treatment within the European Community but not in the UK.' Three weeks later, the HFEA, following the Court of Appeal ruling, allowed Mrs Blood to go to Brussels to have the treatment that enabled her ultimately to have two sons.

This court ruling means that, today, if anyone wants his sperm stored for future use, including use after his death, he must sign a consent form. Also, there is a limit to how long the sperm may be stored – usually only for 10 years.

A particular case where the storage of sperm is important is when a man has cancer treatment – particularly treatment for testicular cancer – and might become infertile. It is usual in such cases to offer a man the opportunity to have some of his sperm preserved before treatment. Then, if he is later found to be infertile, he can still father children.

in Mrs Blood's case – even though Mr Blood's sperm should not have been removed without his permission. The judges said: 'Mrs Blood

SUMMARY

1   Although most people want to have children, 10 per cent of couples cannot conceive naturally.

2   Artificial techniques to assist conception have been available since 1978. These are AIH, AID and IVF.

3   AIH (artificial insemination by husband) is where sperm is taken from the man and implanted in the woman's uterus. Although conception is 'artificial', the couple involved are the genetic parents. Roman Catholics reject this as 'unnatural interference' in the reproductive cycle.

4   AID (artificial insemination by donor) is when the woman is fertile but her partner is not; donor's sperm replaces his and is implanted in the woman's uterus. Only the mother has a genetic relationship to the child but couples often regard this as

preferable to adoption. It is accepted by the Church of England but rejected by Roman Catholics as amounting to adultery (but there is no intimate relationship as there is in adultery).

5   IVF (*in vitro* fertilization) involves fertilizing an ovum (egg) *in vitro* ('in glass'), that is, in a Petri dish. The fertilized ovum is returned to the woman's uterus. The fertilized ovum is not genetically different from the ordinary product of sexual intercourse; it gives otherwise childless couples the chance of children. Roman Catholics object because it separates procreation (making the child) from ordinary marital relations.

6   IVF often produces 'spare' embryos. The law permits genetic research on these up to 14 days after fertilization.

(a) The Roman Catholic Church objects to this as it believes that life begins at conception and that such experimentation on, and later disposal of, spare embryos involves the taking of human life.

(b) The Church of England accepts such research on the grounds that an embryo created by sexual intercourse might not settle in the mother's womb, might divide, become identical twins or even triplets – its future is not set.

GOING DEEPER

7 *Evangelium Vitae*, the encyclical of Pope John Paul II, objects to artificial techniques of reproduction. They

- are 'threats against life';
- separate procreation from conjugal sex;
- produce short-lived embryos; often fail;
- reduce human life to the 'level of "simple biological material"' because of the production of 'spare embryos'.

8 The Anglican Church believes that sperm and egg donations are acceptable as they help people to have children. Although worthy of respect, embryos are not persons; they are like the product of early miscarriages. Therefore, making 'spare embryos' and carrying out research up to 14 days after their creation is permissible. IVF, AID and AIH are all acceptable methods of creating new life.

9 The Human Fertilisation and Embryology Act 1990 (HFEA 1990) prescribes what treatment is permissible.

10 The practical enforcement of the Act's provisions is regulated by the Human Fertilisation and Embryology Authority (also HFEA). This Act has been revised since 1990 to accommodate developments in reproductive technology.

11 The HFEA provides clinics with guidelines to help them to practise legally in accordance with the Act. These guidelines presume that treatment should be offered unless there is evidence that the child is 'likely to experience serious harm'.

 REVISION QUESTIONS

1 What do the initials (the acronym) IVF stand for?

(a) Why might IVF be necessary? (b) Which Christians object to it and why?

2 What do the initials AIH stand for?

(a) Why might AIH be necessary? (b) Which Christians object to it and why?

3 What do the initials AID stand for?

(a) Why might AID be necessary? (b) Which Christians object to it and why?

4 For how many days after conception is it legal to experiment on an embryo?

(a) Which Christians object to this and why?

(b) Which Christians agree to such experiments and why?

GOING DEEPER

5 Name an important Roman Catholic document concerning these issues.

(a) Give three reasons from this document for opposing artificial reproduction.

(b) How does John Habgood, an Anglican and a former Archbishop of York, treat these issues differently?

Personal stories

Carol was not sure when she became pregnant. She had run out of birth control pills but she and her husband, Joe, had used condoms every time they had sex. She never expected to become pregnant and only found out because she had an unrelated health problem, which took her to the accident and emergency (A&E) department late one night. Carol was treated for her health problem but routine tests carried out in A&E revealed that she was pregnant. Shocked, she returned home.

Carol and Joe had different attitudes to continuing with the pregnancy. They'd had to move in with Carol's parents when Joe had lost his job. Carol couldn't bear the thought of living with them *and* having a baby. But Joe wanted to

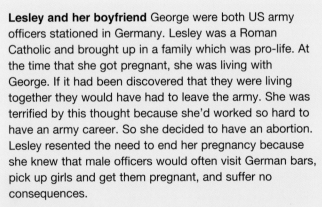

Copyright © Shutterstock

have the baby and he was convinced that God would help them to cope. Since they couldn't agree, time passed and having a medical **abortion** (taking an 'abortion pill') ceased to be an option, so Carol had a surgical abortion. She found the experience a mixed one: the people she dealt with were pleasant and professional but the procedure was painful. Although she felt sad afterwards, she was even more relieved that she didn't have to bring up a child at the wrong time in their lives.

Lesley and her boyfriend George were both US army officers stationed in Germany. Lesley was a Roman Catholic and brought up in a family which was pro-life. At the time that she got pregnant, she was living with George. If it had been discovered that they were living together they would have had to leave the army. She was terrified by this thought because she'd worked so hard to have an army career. So she decided to have an abortion. Lesley resented the need to end her pregnancy because she knew that male officers would often visit German bars, pick up girls and get them pregnant, and suffer no consequences.

Lesley found the experience of the abortion itself very traumatic: 'I had the abortion, and remember listening to

the vacuum machine, and to the nurse asking if all the parts were collected. I came home cramping from the medicine they had put in my IV drip, and crying from the trauma of it all.'

Lesley later had a relationship with a man to whom she got engaged. Her relationship with her fiancé became troubled but nevertheless she decided to get married. She wouldn't sleep with her fiancé unless their relationship was 'legal'. She became pregnant six months after the wedding and had a child a year after her first (aborted) pregnancy. Then her marriage 'died' and she filed for divorce.

Today, she deeply regrets having an abortion. She says: 'God could have directed my life if I had chosen life instead of death for my child.'

Discussion

- If you or (if you are male) your partner had an abortion, how do you think you would feel about it?
- Do you think that your gender (whether you are male or female) affects your attitudes?
- How would you react to someone telling you that she'd had an abortion?

Glossary

abortion the premature ending of a pregnancy; often used to mean the deliberate (medical or surgical) ending of a pregnancy

euthanasia literally 'happy death', i.e. bringing about someone's death because there is little or no quality of life

foetus the unborn baby developing in the womb

pro-life the view that the protection of the life of the foetus should be the main priority

pro-choice the view that the protection of a woman's right to choose what she does with her own body should be the main priority

quality of life the degree of goodness or excellence of life, which can be difficult to measure because different things matter to different people (e.g. the value they place on mobility or enjoying food)

sanctity of life life is of special value because it is the gift of God (the word sanctity is related to the Latin word for holy, *sanctus*, which is one of the qualities of God)

viable capable of surviving

Scientific points

- A fertilized ovum (egg) is genetically unique.
- Fertilization does not happen immediately after intercourse (which is why some regard the 'morning after pill' as morally acceptable).
- Not all fertilized ova continue to develop into foetuses.
- Some foetuses abort naturally (miscarry) in the early stages of pregnancy (up to 1 in 8 according to recent statistics).
- Although a single complete individual may be genetically present at conception, the emergence of the 'person' takes time.
- There is considerable disagreement about when a 'person' emerges in the process of foetal development. Also, of course, we continue to develop as persons long after birth.

INTRODUCTION AND MAIN POINTS

When does life begin?

The reason abortion causes debate is that people disagree about when life begins. Some believe that it begins at the moment that a sperm fertilizes an egg; others believe that life begins much later. If you believe that life begins at fertilization, you are more likely to object to abortion because you will regard it as 'taking a life'. If you believe that the beginning of life occurs later, you might accept that sometimes stopping the development of a fertilized egg by abortion could be a wise course, or at least, the lesser of two evils.

Deciding when life begins is a different matter for us compared with our ancestors. They had no idea about the complex process by which sperm fertilize eggs and genetic material from both parents combines to produce a unique human being.

The ancient world could only speculate about when a person's life began. The Greek philosopher Aristotle (384–322 BC) believed that life began when the soul was implanted. For a male baby the soul was implanted at 40 days and for a female baby at 80–90 days.

Through developments in science and technology, we know much more about what happens from conception onwards. We are familiar with pictures of the development of the **foetus** in the womb. However, there is still disagreement about when a person's life begins. Many Roman Catholics believe that a soul is implanted at conception and that a unique human life begins then (see the *Catechism of the Catholic Church*, paras 2270 and 2273). Others claim that the decisive moment comes when the brain stem is formed.

Why do we exist?

Just as abortion is related to the question of when life begins, it is also related to the purpose of life.

A religious view

For Christians, God brought the universe and human beings into existence because he wanted us to exist. Moreover, human beings are very special because they are made in the image of God (Genesis 1.27). Human life, therefore, is something willed by God – a gift from God – and sacred. Christians refer to this understanding of the sacredness of life as the **sanctity of life**.

If you believe that each human individual is special in the eyes of God (i.e. you believe that each life is sacred from its beginning), you will probably also believe that ending a life would offend God. For similar reasons, abortion is strongly discouraged in Muslim teaching.

A non-religious view

On the other hand, if your view is that human existence is a matter of chance – only a random product of evolution – you might still value it but not because ending a life would 'offend God'. You might believe that it is better to end pregnancy in some cases, such as when the life of the mother is threatened.

Even if you regard human existence as the product of chance, you might regard it as remarkable, as something that humans alone in the universe are aware of and can reflect upon. Because of this perspective, you might place a high value on human life – an essential part of the belief system called *humanism*.

Unwanted pregnancy: the abortion option

Bringing up children is one of life's most demanding tasks but it gives most parents happiness and fulfilment. But becoming a parent in the wrong circumstances can be disastrous, since you become responsible for the life of a person whom you never wished to bring into existence.

For the woman comes a complete change in her body's functioning and the responsibility for another life. For the man, there is the prospect of a legal responsibility to care for the child.

Since 1967 in the UK, abortion – a medical termination – has been an option for a woman who does not want to continue with a pregnancy. But this decision is not necessarily easy: practical or ethical reasons (or a mixture of both) may influence the woman who has become pregnant; and she and the man who made her pregnant might not agree about what to do.

At the heart of the decision will be the balance between the mother's interest and the foetus's interest. To decide this, you have to weigh sanctity of life against **quality of life** (although the people involved in the decision might not use these technical terms).

The purpose of life according to Roman Catholic teaching

To come to God
According to Roman Catholic teaching, the purpose of human life is to come to God: 'a man is bound to follow his conscience in order that he may come to God, the end and purpose of life'.

(Pope Paul VI, *Declaration on Religious Freedom* (Dignitatis Humanae))

To be fruitful
The creation of the world and of human beings was an act of God's love. The love between a man and a woman mirrors this love: 'their mutual love becomes an image of the absolute and unfailing love with which God loves man'. Furthermore, this love should be fruitful: 'And this love which God blesses is intended to be fruitful and to be realized in the common work of watching over creation: "And God blessed them, and God said to them: 'Be fruitful and multiply, and fill the earth and subdue it.'"'

(*Catechism of the Catholic Church*, para. 1604)

Sanctity of life

Those who put sanctity of life first believe that the foetus is a human life from the moment of conception and it should be treated with the same respect as the mother. Unless there is serious risk to the mother's life, they regard the preservation of the foetus's life as more important than the comfort or convenience of the mother. This view is often called **pro-life** because of its emphasis on the value of life.

> **Pro-life** 'Nobody has a right to bring about the death of an innocent human. Killing can never be part of a just policy of care. Nearly 6 million preborn children have been killed under the 1967 Abortion Act – six times the total British dead of the two World Wars.'
>
> (Pro-Life Alliance manifesto; http://www.politicsresourcesnet/area/uk/ass03/man/prolife.htm)

Quality of life

Those who put quality of life first give great weight to threats to the physical or mental health of the mother, or to her general quality of life. It does not mean that they ignore the *potential* quality of life of the foetus. However, a foetus's life is of secondary importance because it is still only a developing life, unlike the mother's, which fully exists. Since this view focuses on choices that the mother has to make, it is often called **pro-choice**.

> **Pro-choice** 'Women cannot manage their fertility by means of contraception alone. Contraception fails, and couples fail to use it effectively.'
>
> (Ann Furedi, Director of Communications, British Pregnancy Advisory Service, the UK's largest abortion provider)

Both pro-life and pro-choice are terms that tend to be used as slogans, with the objective of influencing our opinions and feelings. No one wants to be against either 'life' or 'choice'. When we read the literature of the organizations that support or oppose abortion, we should be alert to the mixture of fact and opinion that they contain. This topic can arouse violent feelings and has even led, in the USA, to the death of doctors who perform abortions.

Pro-choice campaigners outside Dublin's High Court, May 2007

Discussion

'On Friday night, 23 October 1998, Dr Slepian was murdered in his kitchen, shortly after he and his family had returned from Shabbat (Jewish Sabbath) evening services. Dr Slepian was a gynaecologist and obstetrician, a fertility specialist who delighted in delivering babies. He also, as part of his commitment to providing total health care to his patients, performed abortions.'

('Illuminata', the Clergy for Choice newsletter)

Questions

- Why would pro-choice supporters talk about assassination?
- Would you be prepared to demonstrate violently about a moral question (e.g. abortion or animal rights)?

When does the law permit abortion?

Before we look at the main arguments for and against abortion in detail, it is useful to be clear about what the law is in the UK.

Abortion has been legal since 1967 but the law underwent significant reform in 1990 (The Human Fertilisation and Embryology Act, 1990). Since 1990, abortions may normally only be performed on foetuses up to the 24th week of pregnancy. Previously, they were permitted up to the 28th week, but advances in the care of premature babies had made that too high a limit as many foetuses younger than 28 weeks were found to be **viable**.

Abortion is legal until the 24th week of pregnancy if two doctors agree that:

1 continuation of the pregnancy would involve a greater risk to the pregnant woman's physical or mental health than that entailed in having an abortion; or

2 continuation of the pregnancy would involve a greater risk to the physical or mental health of any existing children of the pregnant woman than that entailed in having an abortion.

Abortion is legal at any stage of pregnancy if:

1 doctors agree that continuation of the pregnancy puts the mother's life at risk;

2 an abortion is necessary to prevent grave permanent injury to the pregnant woman's physical or mental health; or

3 there is a substantial risk that the child might suffer from 'such physical or mental abnormalities' as to be seriously disabled.

The main arguments for and against abortion

Arguments in favour of abortion

A woman's body is hers to do with as she likes

Some argue for abortion simply on the grounds that a woman has a right to do whatever she likes with her own body. She has no obligation to bear a child that she does not want.

Some women use this argument even though they accept that a new life has begun at conception:

'abortion supporters say, "This is my body, so don't interfere with it. It's mine, I can do what I want, even to the point of killing the life within it. All is secondary to my dominion over my body". In fact one abortion supporter has written, "I say their [pro-lifers'] God is worth nothing compared to my body".'

(Michelle Goldberg, 'Rant for Choice' (University of Buffalo, New York, student newspaper, 1995); www.catholic.com/thisrock/2000/0009fea4.asp)

The law protects us from physical and mental harm – unwanted pregnancy risks physical and mental harm

The law already provides protection for our physical safety (e.g. there have to be fire escapes and food has to be prepared safely) and mental safety (e.g. against sexual harassment or bullying). Therefore, since unwanted pregnancy can affect a woman's physical or mental safety, she has a right to protection against it. This view is particularly true when a woman becomes pregnant against her own will, as can happen in the case of rape.

Medical risks

Pregnancy can give rise to 'medical risks'. A woman's physical or mental health might be badly affected. There might also be medical risks to the foetus, such as genetic disorders passed on by the parents (e.g. haemophilia or cystic fibrosis), the age of the mother (e.g. the risk of having a baby with Down's syndrome increases as a woman ages) or if the mother is ill (e.g. with rubella, also called German measles). A woman should have the right to avoid these risks.

Pregnancy has negative effects on the way women are treated

Although pregnancy can give women great joy and make others admiring and considerate (for instance, giving up seats for pregnant women on crowded buses and trains), pregnancy can also have a negative effect on a woman's life in society.

- Having a baby might disrupt her education or career.
- She might be unmarried and belong to a family with religious beliefs strongly opposed to sex outside marriage, which means that she could be treated as an outcast in her parents' social world.

Pro-life and pro-choice supporters in front of a women's clinic

Copyright © Press Association

- She might be regarded as 'too young' or 'too old' to have a baby. For example, she might still be at school or be a mature woman with grown-up children.
- She might be unemployed, live in poor housing, have no home or be too poor to raise a child.
- She might be at risk of violence or abuse at home from a husband, partner or family who do not welcome her pregnancy.
- She might lack support at home (e.g. because she is a single parent or does not have a family to help her bring up a child).

 Discussion

'Abortion was legalized in the UK to protect women from illegal 'back-street' abortions, which killed some and left others unable to have children. It was intended to be a 'last resort'. However, the statistics indicate an extraordinary increase in its incidence in the last 30 years. For example, of all pregnancies, the following percentage ended in abortion: 2.8 per cent in 1967; 14.7 per cent in 1977; 17.8 per cent in 1987; 20.9 per cent in 1997; 21.8 per cent in 2004.'

(www.johnstonsarchive.net/policy/abortion/ab-unitedkingdom.html)

Question

- Is this the result of abortion becoming more acceptable (by 1990, 42 per cent of women of child-bearing age had experienced an abortion), poor sex education and/or inadequate use of contraception?

What happens if the life of the mother is affected? The law of 'double effect'

For Roman Catholics, abortion remains a mortal sin even if the life of the mother is threatened. However, Roman Catholics may apply the principle of *double effect*. This recognizes that an action may have a number of different results, of which only one was intended. For example, in war time a bomb may be dropped on an enemy base and, inadvertently, kill a civilian delivering groceries. This is forgivable since the civilian's death was not intended. The motive for action is considered more important than the action itself. Similarly, when applied to abortion, the motive of a doctor or surgeon is what counts. So, if a doctor or surgeon treats a pregnant woman with a life-threatening illness with the intention of saving her life and a foetus dies as a 'side effect' or 'secondary effect' (hence law of 'double' effect), that is permissible. The death of the foetus was not the primary intention and, therefore, not 'contrary to the moral law'. On the other hand, critics of this approach will argue that the surgeon, pregnant woman, and all concerned know that the abortion of the foetus would be an inevitable consequence of the surgeon's action, so it is questionable whether it can be seen as a separate (i.e. 'double') effect.

- She might be an alcoholic or drug addict, which could affect her ability to look after a baby.

- She might already have a large family and not be able to cope easily with another child.

Arguments against abortion

Sanctity of life

Although the Bible contains no specific teaching about abortion, opponents of abortion often claim that biblical teaching about the sanctity of life implies that abortion is wrong.

Their argument follows these steps:

1 People should respect the sanctity of human life. They quote a number of biblical texts to back up the arguments that human beings are made in the image of God (Genesis 1.27) and are individually valued ('even the hairs of your head are all counted', Matthew 10.30), and that life should not be taken ('You shall not murder', Exodus 20.13).

2 They show that Christians have been against abortion from earliest times, in particular quoting from the *Didache* (meaning 'teaching'), a collection of teachings for new Christians, written in about AD 100, which includes the saying: 'You shall not kill by abortion . . .'

3 Taking human life is wrong. Indeed, doing so is usually regarded as murder or manslaughter.

4 Since human life begins at conception, and will afterwards develop into a baby, abortion ends a human life. Abortion should be regarded as murder or manslaughter because, once a foetus is conceived, it will usually develop into a baby capable of being born.

'A woman told how she is to sue the NHS over the psychological trauma she claims to have suffered after having an abortion.'
(*PA News*, 12 June 2002)

A young campaigner displays a pro-life placard

Copyright © Press Association

A demonstrator holds a pro-choice sign amid opponents

or pressure to perform euthanasia on frail people (the old or severely disabled). If we accept the murder of 'imperfect' foetuses, we shall come to accept the murder of people who are already born.

Babies aren't unwanted

The concept of 'unwanted babies' is false. They may be unwanted by their natural parents but there are many infertile couples who would be happy to adopt them. Those who hold this view argue that many 'unwanted' babies were adopted before abortion was legalized in 1967.

Contraception

Principal ethical problem

Contraception raises some of the same ethical problems as abortion. If the form of contraception used involves stopping the development of life even in its earliest stages, those with a pro-life perspective will object to it because its use would entail the loss of life.

However, critics of the pro-life perspective on contraceptive methods would argue that the

Physical and mental ill effects

Abortion can leave a woman less able, or unable, to have a child later on. It may also affect her psychologically. For example, she might believe that she has killed her own child, which could cause depression or other mental illness.

Bad effect on society in general

Some fear that abortion should be considered not only on how it affects a particular woman or couple but also on how it affects society in general. They claim that failure to respect the life of foetuses, at whatever stage of their development, contributes to a general lack of respect for the sanctity of life. Pope John Paul II taught that this attitude leads to a 'culture of death', where there is little respect for life at its earliest stages (abortion) or at its latest (**euthanasia** – see Topic 10) and a readiness to risk human life in war and violence.

The slippery slope

A variation of this argument is that being prepared to take life soon after conception is part of a *slippery slope*. This stance could lead to the routine abortion of 'imperfect' foetuses

Different contraceptive methods

Contraceptive methods divide into those that work by preventing fertilization and those that operate after fertilization.

Preventing fertilization
The contraceptives that prevent fertilization include condoms, a low-dose combined oral contraceptive (COC) and Depo-Provera given by regular injection.

After fertilization
Contraceptives which may operate after fertilization include intrauterine contraceptive devices (IUCDs, 'the coil'), the progestogen-only pill (mini-pill) and contraceptive implant methods (e.g. Norplant).

development of the fertilized embryo into a foetus is not inevitable. It may, for instance, only develop into a mass of cells. Therefore, interrupting its development is no different from what can happen naturally.

To decide if a particular contraceptive method would satisfy a pro-life perspective involves knowing whether it would destroy life after fertilization or simply prevent fertilization.

However, Roman Catholic teaching condemns *any* form of artificial contraception, even if it only prevents fertilization. The basis of this perspective is that preventing fertilization is wrong because it frustrates the primary purpose of sexual intercourse, which is to be 'open' to the production of life.

Critics of this view, though, argue that sex is not only for reproduction. It is also for sustaining marriage, and that couples suffer if they cannot control the size of their families.

Anglican teaching

The Christian Churches have been opposed to contraception for most of the past 2,000 years. However, change began early in the twentieth century. Initially Anglicans (the worldwide family of churches related to the Church of England) were opposed. In 1908, a large conference of bishops from all over the world meeting at Lambeth (the home of the Archbishop of Canterbury) voted against it. However, at the 1930 Lambeth Conference, the bishops voted in support of contraception for married couples. Other Protestant churches followed suit in the succeeding decades. By the 1958 Lambeth Conference, Anglicans had decided that God wanted couples to choose the size of their families.

Roman Catholic teaching

The only kind of contraception that the Roman Catholic Church allows is 'natural family planning', which entails:

The teachings of Pope Paul VI and Pope John Paul II

Pope Paul VI issued *Humanae Vitae* in 1968. This publication forbade all methods of artificial birth control. Many Roman Catholics were surprised by this approach. They had expected the Pope to allow some forms of birth control. Their response was often to ignore his teaching.

Pope John Paul II, even before he was Pope, had written about the importance of the issue of contraception, describing it as a 'struggle for the value and meaning of humanity itself' (*The Anthropological Vision of* Humanae Vitae, 1978). As Pope, he repeated the Church's teaching: 'the natural regulation of fertility is morally correct; contraception is not morally correct'.

- abstention – not having sex (100 per cent effective);
- rhythm method – having sex at the time in a woman's menstrual cycle when she cannot conceive (85 per cent reliable);
- body function method – checking temperature and mucous patterns to estimate when fertility is low and only having sex then (98 per cent reliable).

Natural family planning is the only form of contraception acceptable to the Roman Catholic Church because it uses a God-designed mechanism; it relies on the unique and God-given human characteristic of self-control; it does not completely prevent conception (it remains slightly 'open' to new life); and it adds nothing artificial to sex.

Roman Catholic practice

Despite the Church's official teaching, a majority of Roman Catholics in England and Wales practise artificial contraception. A survey conducted by the Catholic weekly *The Tablet* in 2008 indicated that 54.5 per cent used the contraceptive pill and 69 per cent had used or would be willing to use condoms. Also, more than half of 18–45-year-olds cohabited before marriage, which goes against church teaching that sex should take place only within marriage.

 **GOING DEEPER**

What happens during an abortion?

- A woman receives a general anaesthetic which also affects the foetus so it feels nothing. The neck of the womb is enlarged and the contents of the womb are removed by vacuum aspiration (they are sucked out). The larger pieces of foetal tissue (e.g. the head) are crushed and pulled out with forceps. The foetus's life will end when its head is crushed.

- Very late abortions may entail giving the woman prostaglandin to induce labour. The life of the foetus is first ended with drugs before it is delivered in the same way as a living baby.

- A pill (RU486) can be used to induce abortion in the first ten weeks of pregnancy. It has to be administered under specialist care to ensure that it works properly. The foetus is born dead as it is too underdeveloped to breathe and sustain its own life.

What the Churches teach about abortion

The Christian Churches vary in what they teach but none is in favour of abortion. Some simply have a more sympathetic view towards a woman who perceives her situation as difficult or impossible and, so, permit 'special cases'. The spectrum of opinion varies, as shown in this table.

Roman Catholic	*Absolute*	Abortion is against 'the moral law'. No exceptions even for 'therapeutic' reasons. Never as a means of regulating family size. Teaching is found in *Humanae Vitae* (1968), *Declaration on Procured Abortion* (1974) and *Evangelium Vitae* (1995).
Anglican	*Absolute in principle but allowing rare exceptions*	All human life, including the foetus in the womb, is sacred (General Synod resolution, 1983). Abortion is 'a great moral evil' (Board for Social Responsibility (BSR), 1980). So the basic Anglican view is the same as the Roman Catholic one. But Anglicans recognize some rare exceptions: 'We do not believe that the right to life . . . admits of no exceptions whatever; but the right of the innocent to life admits surely of *few exceptions indeed*' (BSR, 1980). For example, such an exception might be when a mother's life is threatened by continuing a pregnancy.
Church of Scotland	*Absolute in principle but allowing rare exceptions*	'Abortion has no moral justification and represents the unwarranted destruction of human life that is made in the image of God' (Board of Social Responsibility, 1987). *But* this is only applicable in 'the great majority of cases'.
Quaker	*Variety of views accepted*	There is no single view about when a person becomes a person or whether abortion is permissible. It is a matter of personal conscience. Some – relying on the Quaker belief that force should not be used – regard abortion as a wrongful use of force against a person. Others emphasize the right of women to a full role in society. Some also believe that a woman is justified in having an abortion if continuing with a pregnancy might prevent her from achieving her full role (see http://qfp.quakerweb.org.uk/qfp22-54.html or *Quaker Faith and Practice*, ch. 22, subsections 22.54–22.59).

But not all Christians within a denomination have the same view

Church leaders sometimes speak out in favour of avoiding too absolute a position.

For example, Gordon Linney, Archdeacon of Dublin, a Church of Ireland priest (the Church of Ireland is in communion with the Church of England), said: 'It is difficult to believe that there is anyone on this island [Ireland] who is totally anti-abortion, no matter how devoted to the protection of unborn life. There is agreement today, for example, on the commitment to save the life of a mother threatened by physical illness. The question is therefore not whether abortion is morally acceptable but when. It is a matter of where one draws the line.'

Premature babies

Babies can now survive after as little as 22 weeks of pregnancy. This 'lower limit' may continue to be extended, although the more premature a baby is the greater the risk of abnormality in later life.

It was this tendency – for foetuses to survive premature birth earlier and earlier – that led to a change in the law in 1990, reducing the time limit of abortion from 28 weeks to 24 weeks.

Tests for foetal abnormality and their consequences

Increasingly, tests for establishing that something is wrong with a foetus have become more accurate. This strengthens the case of those who support abortion on health grounds (i.e. the health of the foetus but also its impact on the mother's ability to cope).

Two of the most common are ultrasound and amniocentesis.

Ultrasound
It is normal medical practice to perform an ultrasound scan on a pregnant woman's uterus (womb). Since the scan relies on images produced from passing very high frequency sound waves into the womb, it is usually regarded as non-invasive and safe, though there is some – disputed – evidence that this is not the case. It is used to reveal:

- whether the foetus is developing normally;
- the foetus's gender;
- whether there is more than one foetus in the womb.

Information provided in this way may be used to determine whether to continue the pregnancy.

Amniocentesis
This test involves taking a small sample from the amniotic fluid that surrounds the foetus in the womb. It involves some risk but is routinely offered to older women as a means of detecting genetic abnormality, which is a risk when women become pregnant in later life.

Making a decision based on the test
Those who request an abortion on the basis of results from such tests might accept either abortion in general or abortion in 'special circumstances'. They tend further to justify their actions by pointing to the distress and long-term problems that the birth of a child with disabilities might give them and their families. They also argue that many disabled people live in poor conditions, especially in later life when their parents are no longer able to care for them.

However, opponents of abortion on the grounds of disability question whether a life affected by disability should be regarded as necessarily an 'unworthwhile' life, or whether a life should be ended simply because its quality would be poor. After all, they argue, the lives of disabled or elderly people are not ended just because they appear to be of poor quality.

There is also the question of whether any one person can adequately assess the quality of another person's life (e.g. a young athlete might regard the life of a housebound person as worthless but the housebound person might be quite content).

⊚ SUMMARY

1 Abortion in ordinary usage means deliberately causing the death of a foetus and its expulsion from the womb.

2 Abortion is legal in the UK until the 24th week of pregnancy, provided that two doctors agree that continuation of the pregnancy puts the mother's mental or physical health (or that of any of her existing children) at greater risk than would be entailed in having an abortion.

3 Abortion is legal at any stage of pregnancy if the mother's life is at risk, if her physical or mental health risks grave injury, or the child might suffer serious physical or mental disability.

4 Supporters of abortion argue that:

(a) a woman has a right to decide what to do with her own body;

(b) a woman whose physical or mental health might be affected has a right to terminate the pregnancy;

(c) medical risks to the foetus justify abortion. Examples include the risk of the mother's illness affecting the foetus's development (German measles, alcohol or drug addiction), genetic disorders being transmitted to the foetus (e.g. haemophilia or cystic fibrosis) or the mother's age (e.g. being over 40) increasing the possibility of foetal abnormality (e.g. Down's syndrome);

(d) 'social threats' to the mother's well-being justify an abortion: disruption of her education; religious prejudice against unmarried mothers; being too young or too old; unemployment; homelessness; the risk of abuse; having a large family to support; or being 'too young' or 'too old' to have a baby.

5 Opponents of abortion:

(a) appeal to the sanctity of life, arguing that it is always wrong to take a life because life is a gift from God;

(b) quote biblical passages in support of this view: human beings are made in the image of God (Genesis 1.27) and are individually valued ('even the hairs of your head are all counted', Matthew 10.30); and that life should not be taken ('You shall not murder', Exodus 20.13);

(c) refer to Christian tradition. For example, to show that Christians have been against abortion from earliest times, they might quote from the *Didache*, which includes the saying 'You shall not kill by abortion . . .';

(d) point to medical risks. Abortion can leave a woman less able or unable to have a child later and it may also cause depression or other mental illness;

(e) argue that easy abortion may contribute to a casual attitude to the value of human life (what Pope John Paul II referred to as a 'culture of death');

(f) claim that the abortion of 'imperfect foetuses' could (coupled with an acceptance of euthanasia) lead us to accept the murder of elderly and disabled people. Therefore, abortion is part of a moral 'slippery slope';

(g) argue that the concept of 'unwanted babies' is false. There are many infertile couples who would be happy to adopt babies that natural parents do not want. Many 'unwanted' babies were adopted before abortion was legalized in 1967.

6 Contraception and abortion pose similar ethical problems. Pro-life campaigners object to anything that prevents the development of life at its earliest stages. Critics argue that development of a fertilized embryo into a foetus is not inevitable, and interrupting development resembles what can happen naturally.

7 The test of whether a contraceptive method satisfies pro-life views is if it destroys life after fertilization or simply prevents fertilization.

8 Roman Catholic teaching condemns any form of artificial contraception because it frustrates the primary purpose of sex – reproduction.

9 Critics of Roman Catholic teaching argue that sex is not only reproductive but is also intended to sustain a relationship.

10 Anglican teaching has accepted artificial contraception since 1930.

GOING DEEPER

11 Abortion techniques include:

(a) sucking the foetus out of the womb; using forceps to remove all the remaining material (a general anaesthetic prevents the woman or the foetus from feeling anything);

(b) inducing labour for very late abortions; the foetus's life is first ended with drugs;

(c) using the pill RU486 to induce abortion in the first ten weeks of pregnancy.

12 The Christian Churches vary in their opinions about when or if abortion might be necessary, but none is in favour of it. Some permit 'special cases'.

13 Babies can survive if they are born as early as 22 weeks, which is why the abortion time limit was lowered from 28 weeks to 24 weeks in 1990. Very premature babies are at greater risk of abnormalities.

14 Tests for abnormality are performed to check the foetus's health and may reveal grounds for abortion if an abnormality is found.

15 Having an abortion on the basis of test evidence indicates acceptance of abortion or abortion in 'special circumstances' (e.g. when there are serious abnormalities and the prospect of a poor quality of life). Opponents of abortion argue that we cannot rate a life as 'unworthwhile'.

 REVISION QUESTIONS

1 What is meant by the term abortion?

2 Explain the terms 'sanctity of life' and 'quality of life'.

3 When was abortion legalized in the UK?

4 When was the law amended?

5 Give one reason why it was amended.

6 Quote two biblical texts used in the argument against abortion and explain the reasons for their use.

7 What does it mean to say that a foetus is 'viable'?

8 What conditions does the law normally require for a woman to have an abortion?

9 Under what circumstances may an abortion be performed at any stage of a pregnancy?

10 What are the principal methods of artificial contraception?

11 Why does Roman Catholic teaching oppose the use of artificial contraception?

12 What form of contraception is permitted by Roman Catholic teaching?

GOING DEEPER

13 How do two major Christian denominations differ in their official teaching about abortion?

Marriage and sexuality

Personal stories

Adam and Beryl first met when they were in the sixth form. They then went on to the same university, where they are now in their second year. Some of their friends think that it's great they've been together for so long. Others think it's rather 'sad'. Adam's family are Roman Catholic and don't really approve of his living with his girlfriend.

They hope that he will soon get married. Beryl comes from an Anglican family that goes to church now and then, but not regularly. Her parents are easy about Adam living with her but they don't want her to settle down to **marriage** yet. They think that it might get in the way of her career, especially if she has children soon after she's married.

Cheryl has been going out with Dipak for six months and they began to have sex early in their relationship. Cheryl is on the Pill. But, one day, she had a stomach upset which apparently undermined its effectiveness because she has become pregnant. Neither Cheryl nor Dipak wants an abortion but they wonder whether they should be married before the child is born. Cheryl would like a church wedding but Dipak is worried about the expense. Cheryl's family once went to the Methodist church but they aren't really churchgoers. Dipak's family are Hindu.

Elaine is a divorced Roman Catholic mother of two grown-up children. She has been in a lesbian relationship with Florrie for three years and they have lived together for the past two years. Both have well-paid professional jobs. Florrie, a regular member of her Anglican church, is ten years younger than Elaine and has a strong desire to be a parent. Elaine supports Florrie in this and would welcome the responsibility of another child.

A church wedding in Lancing College Chapel

Glossary

adultery a married person having sex with someone other than the person's spouse (wife/husband)

annulment a legal process whereby a marriage is treated as null and void, as if it had never happened

cohabitation living together without being married

consummate to complete a marriage by the first act of sexual intercourse after the wedding

divorce when a marriage contract is ended by court order

heterosexual from the Greek word for 'other', it refers to those people who are attracted to the 'other', i.e. opposite, gender. In colloquial terms, they are known as 'straight'

homosexual from the Greek word for 'like' or 'same'. Homosexuals are people who prefer their own gender sexually. Women who prefer women are often called lesbians but can be called 'gay women'. Men who prefer men are simply known as gay

marriage a man and a woman living together under terms governed by a legal contract, affecting their responsibility for each other's welfare, property rights and the upbringing of children

sacrament a religious ceremony that symbolizes the connection between people and God, and which is seen as a sign of God's grace

Discussion

- Do you think that couples who meet in their late teens are likely to have a lasting marriage?
- Why would a couple want a church wedding?
- If a bride and groom belong to different churches – say, Roman Catholic and Anglican – how should they decide which church to bring their children up in?
- If a woman in a stable relationship finds herself pregnant, should she insist to her partner that they get married?
- Is a civil partnership (a legal relationship between two people of the same sex) the same as marriage?
- Is it desirable that same-sex couples adopt children?

INTRODUCTION AND MAIN POINTS

Marriage no longer has the status it once enjoyed. Two or three generations ago, most men and women expected to be married and to stay married. Today many wonder whether it is worth marrying, partly because so many marriages end in **divorce**. Others prefer simply to live with their partners. However, a majority of people still marry and the main decision that they have to make is whether to marry in church or have a civil (non-religious) wedding.

Many people, especially practising Christians, regret that a large proportion of marriages do not last for life. Some wonder whether it is

too easy to get married and also too easy to get divorced.

Roman Catholics believe that remarriage after divorce is not permitted. Other denominations accept that people make mistakes and should be permitted another opportunity to be married in church.

A notable recent development in the UK has been the provision of civil partnership for couples of the same gender. This reflects an acceptance that a minority of people are attracted exclusively or mainly to their own sex (i.e. they have **homosexual** orientation) and should be given the same legal rights as **heterosexual** (straight) couples.

Civil partnership for gay people is a legal contract but it is not legally the same as marriage, which is only available to heterosexual couples. However, the press often describe civil partnership as 'gay marriage' and it confers basically the same legal benefits as marriage. The Christian Churches assert that marriage can only be between a man and a woman and most of them do not approve of civil partnerships.

Marriage: reasons for and against

The reasons in favour of marriage are practical and, for some, religious.

Marriage as a legal institution establishes:

- shared ownership of property (house, furniture, car, money) and inheritance;
- care of each other (so that one looks after the other in the event of illness and has the right to decide if illness renders the other incapable of decision-making);
- care of children (including looking after them if one parent should die before they are grown up).

Extract from Anglican marriage service

I, *N*, take you, *N*,
to be my wife,
to have and to hold
from this day forward;
for better, for worse,
for richer, for poorer,
in sickness and in health,
to love and to cherish,
till death us do part;
according to God's holy law.
In the presence of God I make this vow.

(*Common Worship: Pastoral Services*)

The language of the promises in the marriage service reflects these needs and, also, the desire that the marriage relationship be permanent.

Religious reasons for marriage

- To allow couples to live together in a relationship characterized by love and mutual support, reflecting biblical teaching (see 'The Christian Egalitarian view', page 48).
- It's the only place for sexual activity.
- For bringing up children.
- Many Christians regard it as a **sacrament**. This belief is the teaching of the Roman Catholic and Orthodox Churches and is widely accepted among Anglicans.

Arguments against marriage

- The view of some feminists is that marriage continues 'patriarchal domination', i.e. that marriage as an institution favours the interests of men over women. For example, in few marriages do men undertake an equal share of responsibility for the children or the care of the home. Thus, women often work as many hours as men but they are also expected to be the main carers of children and the ones who do most of the household chores.
- It is unrealistic for someone to live in an exclusive sexual relationship for the whole of their lives, especially given the far greater longevity that most people can now expect to enjoy.

Cohabitation: living together without being married

Although marriage remains popular, couples are marrying later and choosing **cohabitation** before marriage or opting to cohabit rather than marry.

'**One of the major** changes in family patterns in recent decades, and a contributory factor towards the trend for later first marriage, has been the growth in cohabitation before marriage. Cohabitation prior to marriage was rare in the 1950s and early 1960s (only 2 per cent of those whose first marriage was in the late 1960s had lived with their future spouse before marriage). By the early 1990s more first marriages were preceded with pre-marital cohabitation than not. In addition to the growing proportion of couples living together before marriage there has been an increase in the proportion of people cohabiting, irrespective of whether or not the cohabitation led to marriage. The proportion of all non-married women aged 18 to 49 who were cohabiting in Great Britain more than doubled between 1979 and 1998–99, from 11 per cent to 29 per cent. It is estimated by the Office for National Statistics that there were about 1.6 million cohabiting couples in England and Wales in 1996, and 1996-based projections suggest that the trend towards increasing cohabitation will continue in the future, although the total proportion of people living in couples is expected to fall.'

(www.statistics.gov.uk/statbase)

Arguments for cohabitation

- Women can control their fertility, so there is no reason to marry simply because of the risk of pregnancy.
- 'Living together first' is seen as a way of testing whether marriage would work.
- The couple does not want the legal ties of marriage. If the relationship does not work out, the partners will be able to move on without the complications of the divorce process.

Arguments against cohabitation

- The position of both partners is insecure.
- Children from the relationship might be less well cared for in the event of its breaking up than would have been the case if their parents had been married.
- Cohabitation, with its implication that a couple can go their separate ways if they so choose, is not really a preparation for marriage, which is based on promises being made for life.
- Biblical teaching supports sex within marriage, which means that it is wrong in relationships other than marriage.

Make a pie chart of proportions of people cohabiting versus marrying in the UK based on statistics on this website:
http://www.statistics.gov.uk/STATBASE/ Expodata/Spreadsheets/D7677.xls

Church ceremonies versus civil ceremonies

Since 1837, it has been possible to marry outside the parish church. Today a majority of couples do so. Such weddings without religious ceremony are called 'civil' weddings. In many countries, everyone is obliged to undergo a civil ceremony; those who wish may then have a religious one afterwards.

Arguments for church weddings

- For practising Christians, marriage should be blessed by God.
- They are perceived as 'more traditional' than civil ceremonies.
- They are seen as 'more romantic' than civil ceremonies.

Arguments against church weddings (and for civil weddings)

- Civil weddings are simpler to arrange.
- There is no desire for a religious ceremony.
- The couple does not regard marriage as necessarily lifelong (e.g. all Christian marriage services require a lifelong commitment, although several denominations now permit remarriage).

Equality in marriage

Before 1882, married women could not own property in their own right. When women married, their husbands acquired control over their property. With the introduction of the Married Women's Property Rights Act in 1882, however, married women in England and Wales were given the right to own property.

The twentieth century saw a gradual increase in women's equality: women gained the right to vote, to receive equal pay and to have equal employment opportunities (see the section on gender discrimination in Topic 5).

Christian attitudes to marriage

The justification for subordinating women came from a particular reading of some key biblical texts. Some Christians still hold such views but there is a wide spectrum, ranging from regarding men and women as completely equal in marriage (Christian Egalitarians) – which is how UK law regards married couples – to seeing the man as a having a role of 'headship' to which the woman is subordinate and complementary (Christian Complementarians).

The Christian Egalitarian view

In support of their beliefs, Christian Egalitarians quote passages like that of St Paul to the Galatians (Galatians 3.28): 'There is no longer Jew or Greek, there is no longer slave or free, there is *no longer male and female*; for all of you are one in Christ Jesus'. They interpret this to mean that there is no difference in rights between men and women any longer, any more than there is between Jews and non-Jews, or between free people and slaves. All are equal in their relationship to Christ and therefore to each other. However, whether St Paul could have intended a modern sense of men and women having equal rights is debatable.

Christian Egalitarians also refer to the passage in Genesis, quoted by Jesus: 'Therefore a man leaves his father and his mother and clings to his wife, and they become one flesh.' They believe that the 'one-ness' of man and wife in marriage means that each should be treated in the same way.

The Christian Complementarian view

The Christian Complementarians (whose view is often also described as traditionalist or hierarchical) believe that the Bible requires that men lead and women be subordinate. That is not to deny that they are equal before God but to assert that men and women have different roles in marriage. The man is to lead, provide for and protect his wife and family. Women are to respect their husbands and obey them (hence the promise made by a bride to 'obey' in the older form of the wedding service). A limit to a wife's obedience is set, though, by her not being obliged to follow her husband into sin.

A key passage for Christian Complementarians is Ephesians 5.21–33. However, they tend to extract particular phrases from it rather than read the passage in its entirety. They quote these texts: 'Wives, be subject to your husbands . . . the husband is the head of the wife . . .'. But read the passage for yourself to see how it seems to suggest that obligations between man and wife are balanced. Not only should wives obey but 'husbands should love their wives as they do their own bodies'.

US Southern Baptist teaching about marriage

The Southern Baptists are a conservative, Protestant denomination. Here is some of their teaching about a husband's duties:

'He has the God-given responsibility to provide for, to protect, and to lead his family. A wife is to submit herself graciously to the servant leadership of her husband even as the church willingly submits to the headship of Christ.'

('The family', Article XVIII, *Baptist Faith and Message*)

The husband as 'head': Egalitarian and Complementarian views

It is the meaning of the husband as 'head' that occasions the greatest difference between Egalitarians and Complementarians. Complementarians believe that 'head' means 'authority figure'. Egalitarians believe this concept to be contrary to Jesus' teaching and practice. They quote Jesus' teaching that his followers should not lord it over others in the way that was then customary ('The kings of the Gentiles lord it over them; and those in authority over them are called benefactors. But not so with you; rather the greatest among you must become like the youngest, and the leader like one who serves', Luke 22.25–26).

Egalitarians also argue that the language that Paul uses reflects the culture in which it was written – a culture in which women were treated as men's property and not people in their own right. They also question whether this letter – attributed to St Paul – was actually written by him. If it were not, it is reasonable to question its authority.

Divorce

No marriage over a period of time is likely to be without strains or disagreements. A strong marriage develops when a couple learns to overcome such problems. Indeed, the ability to do so may be seen as one of the most

important routes to developing into a well-adjusted and psychologically mature adult.

However, some couples simply find that they cannot get on with each other. There can be many reasons for this discord. One may discover that the other has been sexually unfaithful or they might simply have become incompatible. In such circumstances, they might seek a divorce.

When couples make the decision to divorce, relatively few will take religious teaching into account because only a minority are likely to be churchgoers. And even if they do react to the Church's teaching about marriage and divorce, they might simply hear it as an example of the Church saying 'no'.

Moreover, many divorced people, especially Roman Catholics, regard the Church as an institution and clergy, in particular, as being out of touch about the reasons for couples wanting to divorce. When asked, divorced people who want to marry again in church think that the clergy are often unsympathetic and lack any real understanding about how much pain failed marriages can cause to couples and, of course, to their children.

Arguments for and against divorce

We should remember how intense the feelings usually are concerning divorce when we read through what can look like a cold, clinical list of 'for' and 'against' arguments.

Arguments in favour of divorce

- If partners become incompatible, the quality of their lives can only improve if they separate.
- If there are children, conflict between parents is damaging for children and divorce will reduce or end the harm that might be done.
- Keeping the promises made in marriage is important but personal happiness is ultimately more important.

Arguments against divorce
- Marriage promises are made for life.
- Children are better off brought up by parents who stay together.
- The break-up of families has an effect on the whole of society. People living on their own after failed marriages often have psychological and practical needs (for example, they might suffer from depression and have housing problems), which society has to address.

Is divorce too easy?

Those who are in favour of easy divorce argue that people who are unhappy in a marriage should not have to cope with an expensive or drawn-out process when they are already unhappy. If they don't want to live together any more, the law cannot make them do so. They should, therefore, be able to 'tidy up' their affairs as easily as possible.

Those who are against easy divorce argue that people are too ready to give up on their marriages. Setting some obstacles in their way should make them try again.

What does the Bible say about marriage and divorce?

Old Testament
In Genesis, woman is depicted as being made from the bone of man. Marriage is seen as

Discussion

- You can get a divorce quite easily, e.g. just by living apart for a time and asking the court for a divorce. But is there such a thing as an *easy* divorce?
- Why do some people fight over the terms of a divorce settlement? Can you think of any famous examples?
- Can divorce be better for a couple's children?

related to this belief: as woman comes from man's 'flesh', so, in marriage, man and woman are 'reunited' in one flesh (Genesis 2.21–23).

However, the Jewish society that produced Genesis also allowed divorce (Deuteronomy 24.1–4):

> Suppose a man enters into marriage with a woman, but she does not please him because he finds something objectionable about her, and so he writes a certificate of divorce, puts it in her hand, and sends her out of his house; she then leaves his house and goes off to become another man's wife. Then suppose the second man dislikes her, writes her a bill of divorce, puts it in her hand and sends her out of his house (or the second man who marries her dies); her first husband, who sent her away, is not permitted to take her again to be his wife after she has been defiled; for that would be abhorrent to the LORD, and you shall not bring guilt on the land that the LORD your God is giving you as a possession.

However, Jewish society regarded **adultery** (Leviticus 20.10) as an offence punishable by death.

New Testament
Jesus' teaching seems to have been in marked contrast to the tradition of his society. In Mark's Gospel, he is quoted as forbidding divorce (Mark 10.2–12). This teaching is repeated in Matthew's Gospel, except that here divorce is permitted on the grounds of adultery (Matthew 5.31–32). Scholars have speculated about whether this teaching reflected Jesus' desire to protect women from the consequences of divorce, i.e. being left without a home or means of support. Perhaps, also, the exception given in Matthew's Gospel reflects its being written later and awareness on the part of the early Christian community for whom it was written that an absolute ban on divorce was not practicable.

St Paul introduced the insight that the relationship between spouses in marriage resembled the relationship between Jesus and the Church (Ephesians 5.21–33).

Current Christian responses

Later Christian tradition has reflected the diversity observable in the biblical texts. Some Churches have forbidden remarriage after divorce (the Roman Catholics and, until recently, the Anglicans) and others have adopted the exception in Matthew's Gospel and previous Jewish tradition to allow divorce and remarriage under certain circumstances.

Same-sex partnerships

There has been considerable debate about whether same-sex partners can marry but, nevertheless, in the UK the government has made civil partnerships possible, which gives same-sex couples much the same rights as married couples.

Civil partnership

In the UK, people of the same sex cannot marry but, since December 2005, when the Civil Partnership Act 2004 became law, gay men and women have been able to register civil partnerships. This Act provides same-sex couples with treatment equal to that of opposite-sex couples who enter into civil marriages (marriages in register offices). This change in the law means that life assurance, employment and pension benefits, wills and inheritance, fatal accident compensation, immigration and nationality matters will be dealt with exactly as in the case of civil marriage. It also means that, if a civil partnership is terminated (as when divorce occurs), there will be the same duty to provide maintenance for a former partner and child support as in a civil marriage.

Arguments for granting same-sex couples equal legal rights to married couples

- Some people have homosexual orientation which leads them to choose a partner of the same sex. Their feelings and needs are indistinguishable from heterosexual couples. Therefore, the same practical reasons that make legal rights of marriage desirable apply (protection of property rights, decisions about the medical care of a loved one, etc.).

- It is unfair for those who may dislike or be opposed to homosexual behaviour to deprive homosexuals of legal security to underpin the promises that they make to each other.

- Permanent relationships are socially desirable and legal rights will encourage gay couples to enter into them.

Arguments against granting same-sex couples equal legal rights

- Homosexual relationships are unnatural and the law should not confer approval on them.

- Granting the same rights to same-sex couples undermines the unique status of marriage.

 GOING DEEPER

The marriage ceremony

The different Christian denominations vary in the way that they perform weddings. However, they all have two principal features in common:

1 vows (legally binding promises) are made;

2 a ring is given or two rings are exchanged.

The couple's vows – reflecting Christian teaching – commit them to a lifelong marriage. The rings exchanged by the couple are themselves 'endless' and express lifelong commitment. The marriage is made a matter of public record by:

- the minister and witnesses signing two registers, and a certificate of marriage that the couple take away with them;

- the return of the marriage details to the Public Record Office.

The Church of England, the Roman Catholic Church and the Orthodox Churches also regard a wedding as a sacrament, i.e. an outward sign of an inward, spiritual reality. The couple's union mirrors the way that the Christian Church is bound spiritually to Jesus by baptism. Also, although there are human witnesses to a couple's promise, God is regarded as the most important witness. In the Church of England, the minister invites the couple to hold hands after they have exchanged their vows. He or she then declares: 'Those whom God has joined together let no one put asunder.'

Roman Catholic Church
In the Roman Catholic Church, the sacrament of marriage concludes with the celebration of a special mass, the nuptial mass. On this occasion, the couple receive communion from each other rather than from the priest: this act symbolizes that, through the Holy Spirit, they are 'in communion' with each other, just as those who receive communion are with Christ.

Orthodox Churches
In the Orthodox Churches, there are quite different customs. The wedding itself is divided into a Service of Betrothal and the Ceremony of the Sacrament of Marriage.

In the Betrothal, the priest blesses rings and then the *koumbaro*, the couple's sponsor (who can be the best man), swaps the rings over between the bride and groom's fingers three times. The fact that this and other rituals (crowning, drinking from the cup and walking round the altar) are performed three times connects the rituals with the blessing of the Holy Trinity: God the Father, God the Son and God the Holy Spirit.

In the Sacrament of Marriage, the priest joins the couple's hands together and they remain joined until the end of the

ceremony, symbolizing the couple's union. During the Marriage, thin crowns, *stefana*, are placed on the couple's heads, joined by a white ribbon. These crowns – symbolizing the glory and honour being given to the couple by God – are blessed by the priest. The *koumbaro* then exchanges the crowns between their heads three times. Following the reading of the story about Jesus' presence at a wedding at Cana in Galilee, when Jesus changed water into wine, wine is given to the couple, which they drink three times. The priest then leads the couple three times round the altar on their first steps as a married couple. After this, the priest blesses them, the crowns are removed and their hands are separated, reminding everyone that only God can end their marriage.

The teaching of the Christian Churches about divorce and remarriage

General
St Paul's teaching about the body being the temple of the Spirit and the need for people to avoid sexual immorality has had a profound effect on the teaching of the Christian Churches, as has St Paul's teaching that it would be better not to be married. Sex has therefore been seen as something that should be confined to marriage and primarily exists for procreation (having babies). Also, the monastic life and the celibacy of the clergy (i.e. unmarried clergy) have been valued by many Christians for most of Christian history. Furthermore, the practical need to provide properly for the upbringing of children and to avoid unwanted pregnancy sustained the traditional view. Changes in the status of women – most women work – and easily available contraception have altered this position.

Roman Catholic Church
The Roman Catholic Church teaches that once a marriage has been made nothing can

undo it: it is indissoluble (it cannot be dissolved). However, if there was something lacking in the couple's promises or, for example, if the marriage is not **consummated** there may be grounds for treating the marriage as 'null and void'. The process of the church authorities granting this is called **annulment** (from the Latin *nullus*, meaning 'none'), treating the marriage as not existing, being 'nothing'.

This practice is often criticized. It is argued that the time-consuming and expensive legal process is something that only well-off people can afford. Also, the grounds for regarding the marriage promises as being flawed (e.g. because someone was too immature to make a promise) may look like seeking an excuse for 'getting round' the fact of the marriage. This approach – of finding any, even unlikely, cause for treating a marriage as a nullity – is an example of *casuistry* (literally 'finding a cause' for a moral choice).

Orthodox Churches

The Orthodox Churches have always accepted that marriages may die and allow for a couple to end such a marriage (in effect to recognize that the relationship has ended) and enter into a second (or, rarely, third) marriage. However, when this happens, less celebration should attend a second ceremony and there should be a prayer of penitence concerning the failure of the first marriage.

Church of England

The Church of England teaches that lifelong marriage is the ideal. However, it now permits its clergy to marry those who have been married before. The decision to do so is left to the discretion of the clergy and they are not obliged to marry people who have had a previous marriage that ended in divorce.

Other Protestant Churches

The Church of Scotland, for example, has for some time permitted a second marriage.

Denomination	Teaching
Roman Catholic Church	Annulment
Orthodox Churches	Death of first marriage, accepts second marriage
Church of England	Remarriage has become possible
Other Protestant Churches, e.g. Church of Scotland	Permit remarriage

Marriage preparation classes

To help couples to prepare for marriage, many churches offer marriage preparation classes. These classes might bring a number of couples together to discuss marriage. They are based on the assumption that couples can benefit from sharing insights and anxieties about the future. Couples who have been married for a time may contribute to the teaching, sharing their experience of the opportunities and difficulties of marriage.

Particular topics might include:

- sexual compatibility;
- coping with conflict and disagreement;
- managing money;
- caring for children.

Linking all these topics will be a reflection on how to recognize and live with the differences of personality, taste and beliefs. A marriage can work well even when the partners have very different temperaments, tastes and beliefs, but success is less likely to happen if they have not come to terms with any differences. Romance may have brought a couple to the point of marriage, but most evidence points to successful marriages resulting from a recognition of these factors and a willingness to 'work at' a relationship.

⦾ SUMMARY

1 The status of marriage has declined but a majority of people still marry.

2 For many couples, the main question is whether to have a church wedding or a civil ceremony.

3 In the debate of church versus civil weddings, church weddings are favoured for being blessed by God, more traditional and more romantic. Supporters of civil weddings value them for being generally cheaper and simpler. They also suit those who do not want a religious ceremony or who do not necessarily want a lifelong commitment (civil marriages can be simply ended by divorce and further marriages entered into).

4 Changing attitudes to sexual orientation have led many to believe that people who are attracted exclusively or mainly to their own sex (i.e. they have homosexual orientation) should have the same legal rights as heterosexual couples.

5 The principal non-religious reasons in favour of marriage are that it grants each person financial rights (e.g. if you have both worked to buy a house, each will have rights in it after a divorce) and it gives a legal framework for the care of children and each other.

6 The religious reasons for marriage are that it reflects biblical teaching, is regarded as the only place for sexual activity and, for some denominations, is regarded as a sacrament.

7 Cohabitation is favoured by many partly because control of fertility means that women need not marry from fear of pregnancy. Some see it as a way of 'testing a relationship', others as a way of avoiding the legal ties of marriage and the complications of divorce if the relationship ends.

8 However, cohabitation is not ideal because of its insecurity, especially if there are children. Also, biblical teaching can be seen as being against sex except in marriage.

9 Many marriages end in divorce. For religious people, there may be a problem concerning remarriage after divorce. For example, unless a marriage is annulled, the Roman Catholic Church does not permit remarriage.

10 Divorce is rarely easy. However, it might be the better choice if the partners are incompatible, if there is a need to protect any children from parental conflict, and for personal happiness.

11 Critics of divorce argue that marriage vows are lifelong; children benefit from a stable home; and marital break-up has social effects (more homes needed, etc.).

12 The argument about divorce is balanced between not obliging the unhappily married to struggle to remain married and not encouraging couples to give up on their marriages too readily.

13 Critics of marriage see it as still favouring the interests of men (a feminist objection) and that our longevity makes it unrealistic for someone to commit to a lifelong exclusive relationship with one other person.

14 Genesis describes marriage as a given 'basic' whereby man and woman become 'one flesh'. However, Jewish law permitted divorce but adultery was punishable by death.

15 Jesus forbade divorce (but allowed it where there was adultery). St Paul saw a couple's relationship as comparable to that between Jesus and the Church. Some take Jesus' presence at the wedding at Cana in Galilee as a sign of his approval of the sacrament of marriage.

16 UK law favours same-sex couples enjoying the same legal rights as married couples. Supporters of this view argue that homosexual and heterosexual lifelong relationships are indistinguishable and that same-sex couples should have the same legal security as married people. Moreover, those who disapprove of homosexuality have no

right to deprive gay couples of such security. Permanent relationships of whatever kind contribute towards a stable society.

17 Critics argue that same-sex relationships are unnatural and that conferring rights on them undermines the uniqueness of marriage.

GOING DEEPER

18 Wedding ceremonies in Christian denominations vary but all have legally binding promises (vows). A ring is given or rings are exchanged as an outward sign of the promises. Registers are signed and witnessed as records of the ceremony. The couple is given a marriage certificate.

19 In the Roman Catholic Church, the marriage is followed by a wedding (nuptial) mass.

20 In the Orthodox Churches, there is a Service of Betrothal (where rings are blessed and swapped three times) and the Sacrament of Marriage, where the couple's hands are continuously joined, symbolizing their lifelong union, and they wear wedding crowns.

21 The Roman Catholic Church regards marriage as indissoluble. However, annulment is permitted (treating the marriage as if it had not occurred). Non-consummation is one reason for annulment. Critics regard some of the other grounds (e.g. psychological immaturity) for annulment as casuistical.

22 The Church of England teaches lifelong marriage as ideal but permits the clergy to marry those who have been married before and subsequently divorced.

23 The Orthodox Churches accept that marriages can 'die' and have always permitted subsequent marriages, provided they include a prayer of penitence.

24 Protestant Churches like the Church of Scotland have permitted second marriages for some time.

25 To help couples to prepare for marriage, many churches offer marriage preparation classes. Topics covered will include sexual compatibility, coping with conflict and disagreement, managing money and caring for children.

REVISION QUESTIONS

1 What is meant by these terms: marriage, divorce, annulment, cohabitation?

2 What are the main non-religious reasons for marriage?

3 What are the main religious reasons for marriage?

4 Give two reasons why many couples cohabit.

5 What was the Old Testament teaching about divorce?

6 What was the Old Testament teaching about adultery?

7 Quote two biblical texts used to support lifelong marriage and explain the reasons for their use.

8 Give two reasons in favour of granting same-sex couples the same legal rights as married couples.

9 Give two reasons against granting same-sex couples the same legal rights as married couples.

GOING DEEPER

10 How do two major Christian denominations differ in their official teaching about remarriage after divorce?

Prejudice and discrimination

 Personal stories

Kwame, 22, has an engineering degree. He has spent his entire life in the UK. His parents arrived here from Ghana 30 years ago. Now that he has finished at university and has a job in London, he wants to rent a flat. He made initial enquiries by telephone with a number of private landlords and then followed his calls up with visits. Three landlords seemed positive on the phone but claimed that the flat had 'already been taken' when he turned up.

Jean, 30, obtained an English degree from Oxford University. After graduating, she joined a merchant bank. She trained alongside a group of mainly male new recruits. Once she'd completed her training, she felt that there was a 'glass ceiling' for women in her rather old-fashioned workplace: men with the same qualifications and of the same age were promoted ahead of her. Now, the banking crisis has led the directors of the bank to make some of its employees redundant. Jean is dismayed to discover that she will be laid off instead of male employees of the same age, who have similar lengths of service and qualifications to her.

Leah, who is Jewish, discovered that she was lesbian when she was in the sixth form. Coming to terms with this was difficult but her family were supportive. Now 26, she has just entered into a civil partnership with Glenys, who is Roman Catholic. Both Glenys and Leah are primary school teachers. They would like to adopt a child but they have been dismayed to encounter **prejudice** from some of the adoption agencies that they have approached, particularly a Roman Catholic one that Glenys contacted.

 Discussion

- Do you think that anyone would be denied a flat or a job today just because they were black or gay?

- Do you think that it matters whether a teacher is gay or not?

- Would you describe yourself as an unprejudiced person?

- Can you describe an incident when someone showed prejudice and discriminated against someone else?

Glossary

discrimination acting on prejudice

ecumenism initiatives on the part of the Christian denominations to achieve greater cooperation and unity

equality enjoying equal legal and political rights, regardless of gender, ethnicity (racial origin) or sexual orientation

evangelism (from the Greek *euangelikos*, 'to bring good news') preaching and spreading the gospel; the gospel is the proclamation that Jesus is the Redeemer – the central belief of Christianity. Matthew, Mark, Luke and John – the four Gospel writers – are also known as the Evangelists

homophobia discriminating against another because of his or her sexual orientation (literally, fear of homosexuals – people who are sexually attracted to others of the same gender)

interfaith dialogue when people of different religious traditions relate to one another and share information and insights about their beliefs

justice the concept of what is right based on law, religion or an ethical system; justice is done when those who act against the system are held to account

missionary (from *mittere*, the Latin for 'to send') a person sent out to do religious or charitable work. The work of a missionary does not necessarily involve converting someone to a faith

positive action measures that aim to prevent discrimination or overcome past discrimination

positive discrimination treating one person more favourably than another because of that individual's gender, race, age, marital status or sexual orientation; unlawful, except in the case of disabled employees or genuine occupational requirement (see page 63)

prejudice having an opinion or belief that has been formed in advance of, without or in spite of relevant evidence

racism discriminating on the grounds of race

sexism discriminating on the grounds of sex (gender)

social injustice occurs when individuals or a society are denied human rights, e.g. equality before the law, freedom of speech and freedom of association – see the Universal Declaration of Human Rights for a fuller definition (www.un.org/en/documents/udhr/index.shtml#atop)

 INTRODUCTION AND MAIN POINTS

We tend to pick up attitudes and beliefs from our parents, our wider family and from our peers (i.e. those with whom we go to school or work), and they are reinforced by daily repetition. Some of these views may be regarded as admirable by most people, e.g. being polite to others, helping those who are vulnerable, working hard or not telling lies.

Which prejudices might either of these groups stir and for whom?

Prejudice

However, we need to recognize that many of our views are 'pre-packaged' and we haven't given them much thought ourselves. Yet this fact doesn't stop us coming to value them when we are older and able to reflect on them. We may later be glad that our families passed on positive attitudes about honesty and hard work. On the other hand, they might have passed on dubious, less worthy attitudes. For instance, attitudes picked up from our families might have encouraged us to look down on people of a different social class, nationality or skin colour. Such unreflecting, pre-packaged ideas are called prejudices. When we act on prejudices, without thinking through what they are based on, or their effect, we discriminate against others.

The reaction of society and government to prejudice on the grounds of gender and colour

In the era after the Second World War, and especially in the 1960s, many of these prejudices came under close scrutiny. Laws were passed in the UK and other countries to prevent many kinds of **discrimination**. The principal UK legislation includes the Equal Pay Act 1970 (EPA), the Sexual Discrimination Act 1975 (SDA), the Race Relations Act 1976 (RRA) and the Disability Discrimination Act 1995/2005.

The Acts have not stopped discrimination but they have marked a change in social attitudes, and the victims of discrimination can use the law to claim their rights.

It is important to note that the legislation deals with discrimination, rather than with prejudice itself.

Forms of prejudice

Prejudice takes many forms, of which prejudice on the grounds of race, gender, religion and sexual orientation are the most common.

Racism: racial prejudice

Racism can be defined as hatred or contempt for people of a different race.

'Race' is often used clumsily and many people confuse it with other factors. For example, some white people think of Jewish people and Muslims as belonging to different races from them when in fact the distinguishing characteristic is culture or religion. Technically, most Jewish people and certain Muslims (of south-east European, Arabian and South Asian origin) are Caucasians and so belong to the same 'race' as white Europeans.

Legislation concerning equal employment rights, race, gender and disability

Equal Pay Act 1970 (EPA)
This statute gives a person a right to the same pay and benefits (pension, sick leave, etc.) as someone of the opposite sex doing the same job, as long as the work is of a similar kind, rated as equivalent and is proved to be of equal value.

Race Relations Act 1976 (RRA)
The principal law concerning discrimination in the UK is the Race Relations Act 1976. It was amended in 2000 and again in 2003, when the EU Race Directive was incorporated into British law. The Act makes it unlawful for a person or public bodies to discriminate against anyone on the grounds of race, colour, or ethnic or national origin.

Sex Discrimination Act 1975 (SDA)
This law resembles those concerning racial discrimination. It forbids sex discrimination against individuals in matters of work, education, provision of goods, facilities and services.

Disability Discrimination Act 1995/2005 (DDA)
This Act, originally passed in 1995 and extended in 2005, aims to promote civil rights for disabled people and to protect them from discrimination in areas such as employment; education; access to many public – and even some private – goods, facilities and services; and buying or renting property. Employers must also make 'reasonable adjustments' – such as improving accessibility to buildings and allowing disabled employees more flexibility with their working hours – in order to promote equality.

The Nazis were prejudiced against Jewish people. To identify Jewish-owned shops, which they often attacked, they painted the word *Jude* on the windows

Some jobs used to be seen as appropriate only for men but these stereotypes have broken down

When people have racist views, they regard those of a different race or culture as inferior in physical, intellectual or spiritual qualities. To some extent, the Nazis, who planned the Holocaust (see Topic 11, page 121), regarded the Jews as less than human. So they believed that their violent discriminatory behaviour towards the Jewish people was permissible.

Sexism: gender prejudice

Sexism occurs when women or men are barred from an occupation or equal pay on the grounds of their gender. For example, 50 years ago very few women entered politics and very few men were nurses.

Historically, sexism has often been directed by men towards women because men have usually been dominant in society. Women's positions may have been weaker for physical reasons and because they bear children. To bear children, women usually have to take a break from work, which might render them less valuable to employers. Also, if they return to work, the need for continued care for their children might lead to a higher level of absenteeism.

Today, though, the majority of women are in work and such discrimination has been legislated against. However, women often

refer to a 'glass ceiling'. By this term they mean that, despite having legal **equality** of opportunity with men in the workplace, equality is denied to them in practice. For example, a woman might find that although she is the best candidate for a promotion, a man is promoted over her, and she can't rise above a certain level (the 'glass ceiling').

Discussion

How would you explain the frequent absence of women from the top in big companies?

'Is the "glass ceiling" for women tougher than ever?

Anglo American, the world's second largest mining group, has named its first ever female chief executive: 49-year-old American Cynthia Carroll.

She becomes the third female chief executive of a FTSE 100 company, joining Dame Marjorie Scardino of media group Pearson and Dorothy Thompson of Drax. It may make her a major power broker in the City, on a million-pound-plus salary, but is she the exception to the rule?

Despite high-profile attempts by the likes of Patricia Hewitt when she was Trade Secretary to get more women in the boardroom, their numbers are dwindling – from 20 in the FTSE in 2005 to 13 this year at the last count.'

('Speakers' Corner', *Daily Telegraph*, 24 October 2006)

Homophobia: prejudice towards homosexuals

Sexual relationships are classed as heterosexual (from the Greek word *heteros*, meaning 'other'), homosexual (from the Greek word *homos*, meaning 'same') and bisexual (derived from the Latin word *ambo*, meaning 'both'). People who are sexually attracted to people of the same gender as themselves are called homosexual or gay.

In the past, there was a lot of prejudice against homosexuals. Today, many people are still more comfortable with the idea of heterosexual relationships than they are with homosexual ones. Even so, they do not necessarily fear or hate people who are gay. **Homophobia**, on the other hand, is the fear or hatred of people who are homosexual and includes the belief that the only acceptable sexual orientation is a heterosexual one.

Homosexual activity between men was illegal until 1967; there was never any law against homosexual (lesbian) activity between women.

Social attitudes and the law have changed considerably since 1967. The age of consent for both heterosexual and homosexual activity is now 16. Many jobs are advertised declaring that they are open to all regardless of gender, race, age or sexual orientation.

However, considerable debate continues within the Christian Churches about the status of homosexual relationships and about whether practising homosexuals can be ordained to church ministry. Some critics see the reluctance of the Christian Churches fully to accept homosexuals as homophobia hiding behind a screen of belief.

Homophobia is far less common in British society than it was before sexual relations between consenting same-sex adults were legalized in 1967. For example, politicians, who depend upon public support to be elected, can be open about their homosexuality in a way that would have been unimaginable in the 1960s or 1970s; some have even served as cabinet ministers. Men and women in the arts and police have also been able to be open about their sexuality. However, professional sport still appears to be relatively homophobic: only a few have 'come out' during their careers; many have not done so until they have retired.

Discrimination against disabled people

About 14 per cent of adults and 3 per cent of children are officially classed as disabled. Of these, a third live in poverty (as officially classified). It can be very difficult for disabled people to receive the help they need, to be properly housed or to be employed. For those with physical disabilities, there can be problems with gaining access to public places (although legislation has resulted in improved access

A wheelchair basketball final at the Paralympic Games. The popularity of the Paralympics, which attracts a large audience of disabled and able-bodied people, reflects the changing public perception of those with disabilities

to public transport and buildings, and the provision of facilities such as disabled toilets).

The term 'disabled' covers three categories:

1 people who are physically disabled;
2 people with learning disabilities;
3 people who are mentally ill.

Fewer people are actively prejudiced towards disabled people than are sexist or racist. However, many would consider that failing to make reasonable provisions for physically disabled people (e.g. installing step-free access to buildings) is a form of discrimination, even if it is 'passive'.

But some people are actively hostile towards disabled people. For example, employers, landlords and transport providers know that improving opportunities and accessibility for disabled people can be complicated and expensive, and may therefore be unwilling to make special considerations.

Other people may harbour an irrational fear or hatred of disabled people, and will deny them certain opportunities simply because they are not 'normal'. The Disability Discrimination Act 1995/2005 makes such behaviour illegal, although in practice it can be difficult to enforce the law. As a result, many disabled people find it hard to get a job.

 GOING DEEPER

What the Churches teach

Roman Catholic Church
In the past half century, promoting the equality of people's treatment, regardless of 'sex, race, colour, social condition, language or religion', has become a keynote of Roman Catholic social teaching, particularly championed by Pope John Paul II (1978–2005). The religious basis for this teaching is

A diverse crowd of people greets the Pope in Yonkers, USA

that every human being is created in 'God's likeness' and should be honoured on that basis. This belief means that no person is valued less than any other, although people's physical, intellectual and moral qualities may vary.

Discussion

Why do you think that Roman Catholic teaching has changed?

Church of England

The Church of England, since it has a parish structure that offers to serve every single person in England, is in a unique position to report on social conditions. In 1985, the report of the Archbishop of Canterbury's Commission on Urban Priority Areas, *Faith in the City*, noted 'that racial discrimination and disadvantage still represent a challenge to be overcome in our society'. The Church's response to this problem should be based on 'compliance with the present laws against direct and indirect racial discrimination' (page 96).

Internationally, the witness of Anglican leaders like Bishop Trevor Huddleston and Archbishop Desmond Tutu was important in the struggle against apartheid in South Africa in the 1960s.

Archbishop Trevor Huddleston (with Nelson Mandela) at a rally

Society of Friends (Quakers)

Quakers have a long and honourable history of opposition to racism. In 1776, the Quakers in Philadelphia prohibited slave ownership in their community. During the 1930s, British and American Quakers tried to prevent the persecution of Jewish people. Quakers were also supporters of, and channels of communication for, black leaders in Southern Rhodesia (now Zimbabwe) and South Africa in the fight to secure the rights of the black majority.

An historic example of resistance to prejudice: Martin Luther King Jr

Martin Luther King Jr (1929–68), an American Baptist minister, became a leading figure in the civil rights movement in the 1950s. In 1955, he became President of the Montgomery Improvement Association, which led a boycott of all buses in Montgomery County, Alabama, by black people for 382 days. This protest was in response to the arrest of an

Martin Luther King Jr at the Lincoln Memorial, Washington, DC, 1963

elderly black woman, Rosa Parks, who refused to give up her seat to a white person.

A highlight of his campaign was the march on Washington in 1963, when 250,000 people (60,000 of whom were white) converged on the capital to demand equal rights for black people and white people, and demonstrated in favour of the Civil Rights Bill then before Congress.

King was often criticized and persecuted during his life. He paid the ultimate price (of martyrdom, many would say) when he was assassinated in 1968.

Positive discrimination

Positive discrimination may be defined as *discriminating in favour* of those who were formerly discriminated against (*The Chambers Dictionary*, 2003). This idea of giving preference to minority or disadvantaged groups over others could be seen as breaking the laws laid out in the Race Relations Act (RRA) and the Sex Discrimination Act (SDA). It is, therefore, important to draw a distinction between positive discrimination and something called **positive action**.

Positive action

Doing something to redress a perceived imbalance is called positive action. Positive action may be defined as taking positive steps to ensure that minority groups and women are *not discriminated against*.

The RRA and SDA allow the giving of opportunities to members of 'under-represented groups'. For example, political parties have tried to increase the number of women in public life by having 'all-women shortlists' for parliamentary candidates.

Under both the RRA and SDA, it is lawful for an organization to provide access to training or to encourage and help members of an under-represented group to undertake a certain type of work, if, at any time during a 12-month period, there is no one of a minority group or gender doing that work within a particular workforce.

Positive action for disabled people

Positive action in favour of disabled people is allowed by the Disability Discrimination Act (DDA), such as providing special facilities for people in wheelchairs or equal job opportunities (see page 60). However, the requirement to make appointments on merit in certain organizations means that some employers cannot discriminate in this way.

Women priests

The SDA grants a 'genuine occupational qualification' to the Christian churches, permitting them to bar women from the priesthood on the grounds of belief.

The Baptist and Methodist Churches, and other independent denominations, which have female ministers, do not take advantage of this exemption. However, the Church of England has ordained women priests only since 1994 and, as yet, has no women bishops.

Neither the Roman Catholic nor Orthodox Churches entertains the idea of women priests.

Women bishops of the Anglican Communion

Copyright © Cynthia Black

Arguments for the ordination of women

1 Although legal, not to ordain women is sexist. More women than men attend church but women are discriminated against as inferior.

2 The Church should demonstrate its inclusiveness by granting men and women equal opportunities of ordination.

3 The priest's role is to represent the whole people of God, male and female, so gender is irrelevant.

4 The Bible, which is authoritative for Christians, was written at a time when the status of women was very different from today's (at least, in Western countries).

5 Although the 12 disciples were men, Jesus had women followers, such as Mary Magdalene, who met him after his resurrection.

Arguments against the ordination of women

1 Jesus chose 12 men as his disciples. If he had wanted to choose women, he would have done so.

2 To depart from the tradition of ordaining only men, all the Churches would have to agree to do so. None has the right to 'go it alone'.

3 When a priest celebrates the Eucharist, he represents Christ, who was male. Therefore, the priest must be male.

Homosexuality and the Church

All the Christian Churches have found difficulty in defining their attitudes to homosexuality, especially towards homosexuals who are members of the clergy. The position of the individual denominations seems to be constantly evolving (see www.cofe.anglican.org/about/gensynod/houseofbishops/humansexualitych5.pdf). At the beginning of the twenty-first century, many Christian denominations permitted the ordination of celibate homosexuals but few allowed ordination for homosexuals in a sexually active relationship.

For example, the Church of England permits the ordination of homosexual men and women as long as they are celibate (not in a sexual relationship). The Roman Catholic Church also appears to permit the ordination of homosexuals (but recent teaching about this is complicated), as long as they are not in a sexual relationship. This approach means that the same rule of celibacy is required of Roman Catholic clergy, whatever their sexual orientation.

However, the Episcopal Church of the USA (TEC) permits the ordination of gays and lesbians as priests – whether celibate or not – as does the Anglican Church of Canada.

Arguments for the ordination of homosexuals

1 Sexual orientation does not affect the ability of men or women to be effective clergy. Many outstanding homosexual men and women have exercised Christian ministry effectively.

2 Jesus never taught about homosexuality.

3 Jesus taught that God regards all human beings as equally valuable.

4 The biblical texts that are used by some to condemn homosexuality are tied to their historical period and do not apply today

The Very Revd Jeffrey John, Dean of St Albans, who is gay, withdrew his acceptance of a bishopric because of opposition from some sections of the Church of England

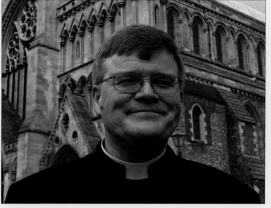

Equality in God's eyes: evangelism, missionary work and ecumenism

'Go therefore and make disciples of all nations, baptizing them in the name of the Father and of the Son and of the Holy Spirit' (Matthew 28.19). In this command to his disciples, Jesus includes everybody regardless of nationality, ability, race, gender or sexual orientation. Inspired by Jesus' words, Christians have taken their faith to all parts of the world. As a result of generations of this **evangelism**, there are over two billion Christians of both sexes and all races, belonging to many different denominations. The Acts of the Apostles and the letters of St Paul in the New Testament describe how this work began.

Evangelism is only one aspect of **missionary** work. Christian missionary work can also involve helping poor and disadvantaged people with literacy and health care, providing orphanages, and assisting with economic development. Missionaries who do such work are behaving like the Samaritan in Jesus' parable of the good Samaritan (Luke 10.25–37), who cared for the wounded man he found by the roadside. Mother Teresa's work among the poor, sick, orphaned and dying in Calcutta – and her founding of the Missionaries of Charity – is a recent example of this type of missionary work.

During the twentieth century, many Christians came to regret that evangelism was carried out by separate denominations. These denominations competed with one another for converts, a practice at odds with Jesus' hope, expressed in John's Gospel, 'that they [his disciples] may all be one' (John 17.21). **Ecumenism** has since become an objective of the major denominations, which have tried to have closer relationships, and to worship and work together on humanitarian projects.

The Church of England has been actively involved in dialogue with other Christian denominations (the Roman Catholic Church, the Orthodox Churches, the Methodists and the United Reformed Church). There has also been interfaith dialogue between the major Christian denominations and other world religions. The Roman Catholic *Declaration on Religious Freedom (Dignitatis Humanae)* (1965) of the Second Vatican Council (see page 135) teaches that every person is free to embrace and profess the religion of his or her choice. Another Second Vatican Council document, the *Declaration on the Relation of the Church to Non-Christian Religions (Nostra Aetate)* (1965) condemns racial and religious prejudice.

(see Leviticus 18.22, Romans 1.26–27 and 1 Corinthians 6.9).

Arguments against the ordination of homosexuals

1 Sexual relationships outside marriage are forbidden for Christians, whether straight or gay (this might mean that celibate gay ministers – i.e. those who are not in a sexual relationship – are allowed to exercise a ministry).

2 The Bible teaches against any sexual relationships which are not heterosexual (involving members of the opposite sex; again, see Leviticus 18.22, Romans 1.26–27 and 1 Corinthians 6.9).

Prejudice towards disability

People with physical disabilities

Physical disabilities may include loss of or injury to limbs, blindness and deafness. In developed countries, most people who are physically disabled cope without help or assistance from the state. Legally, they are entitled to employment opportunities with

larger companies and to receive practical assistance in the form of facilities such as disabled access ramps, loop hearing systems and Braille lettering on signs in public places.

Despite this legal protection, however, disabled people still encounter discriminatory behaviour on a daily basis. For example, an employer, faced with two candidates for a job, may break the law by choosing the able-bodied applicant even if the disabled person is equally well – or maybe even better – qualified than the other person. Even a well-meant action, such as helping someone in a wheelchair to cross the road, can be offensive, since it suggests that the disabled person is in constant need of help and attention from others.

People who are mentally ill

Mental illness is diverse and widespread. Depression is a particularly common disorder that many struggle with at some point in their lives. Significant numbers of people are affected by phobias, such as agoraphobia or claustrophobia; and disorders like schizophrenia and bipolar disorder are severely disabling (see www.mind.org.uk for details). Moreover, old people are susceptible to senile dementia.

There is widespread ignorance surrounding mentally ill people, and this lack of understanding leads to ungrounded prejudices about the threat they pose to society. For example, a 2009 study revealed that, despite widespread opinion to the contrary, mentally ill people are no more likely than 'normal' people to murder a stranger (www.medicalnewstoday.com/articles/167164.php).

The charities SANE and Mind endeavour to dispel the myths surrounding mental illness, and they also constantly put pressure on the government to make better provisions for mentally ill people.

A Christian view of disability

In the Bible, suffering is viewed as a consequence of Adam and Eve's 'original sin', and is thus common to all. Some Christians, however, interpret Jesus' remark, 'Which is easier, to say to the paralytic, "Your sins are forgiven", or to say, "Stand up and take your mat and walk"?' (Mark 2.9) as evidence that Jesus considered physical disability to be a direct result of the individual's wrongdoing. On the other hand, in John 9.1–3 Jesus denies that a certain man is blind because he or his parents sinned; rather, he is blind 'so that God's works might be revealed in him'.

SUMMARY

1 We pick up ideas from families and our peer group. Some of these may be positive but other 'pre-packaged' ideas (prejudices) can be negative, like looking down on people of a different social class, nationality or skin colour.

2 If you act on a prejudice, you are showing discrimination.

3 Many forms of discrimination have become illegal:

   (a) the Equal Pay Act 1970 (EPA) aims to ensure that people doing the same types of work receive the same pay and benefits, regardless of race, colour, or national or ethnic origin;

   (b) the Race Relations Act 1976 (RRA) is designed to prevent discrimination because of race, i.e. it is illegal to refuse to employ people because they aren't white;

   (c) the Sexual Discrimination Act 1975 (SDA) aims to prevent pay discrimination because of gender, e.g. it is illegal to pay a woman less than a man for doing a similar job.

   (d) the Disability Discrimination Act 1995/2005 aims to protect disabled people from discrimination in the areas of employment, education, access to everyday services and property rental.

4 Prejudices about race, gender, religion and sexual orientation are the most common.

5 Racial prejudice – believing that one race is superior to another – is called racism.

6 Prejudice on grounds of gender – believing that men and women are not equal – is called sexism. In the life of the Christian Churches, many claim that not ordaining women as bishops or priests (which neither the Roman Catholic nor Orthodox Churches do) is an example of sexism. However, some argue that, from a theological point of view, women can't be priests.

7 Prejudice about sexual orientation – believing that only heterosexual orientation is acceptable – is called homophobia. Sexual orientation is classed as heterosexual (being attracted to the opposite gender); homosexual (being

attracted to the same gender) and bisexual (being attracted to both genders).

8 Social attitudes have changed since the 1967 Act legalized homosexual acts in private. The age of consent, heterosexual and homosexual, is now 16; jobs are advertised as open to all regardless of sexual orientation.

9 Discrimination against disabled people is often passive, e.g. the failure to provide services or special facilities for them.

10 An example of active hostility towards disabled people would be discrimination in the job market; an employer might refuse to employ a suitably qualified person because he or she is disabled.

GOING DEEPER

11 The Christian Churches – although they may accept that some people have a homosexual orientation – tend to distinguish between orientation and activity. Most accept that someone of homosexual orientation may be ordained (as a priest, minister, etc.) but only a few permit the ordination of sexually active homosexuals.

12 Attitudes to homosexuality depend largely upon approaches to biblical interpretation. Those who accept homosexuals tend to take passages from the Bible and interpret them according to their original historical context; others, however, believe that such texts should be read literally and clearly prohibit homosexual relationships. Yet others argue that Jesus never taught about homosexuality, so there is no specific prohibition from him.

13 Positive discrimination favours people because they belong to an 'under-represented group'. Giving preference to some of these groups over others could be viewed as breaking the Race Relations Act and Sex Discrimination Act but is allowed under the Disability Discrimination Act.

14 Positive action is taking positive steps to ensure that minority groups and women are not discriminated against. It is about helping people to have opportunities from which they might otherwise have been excluded.

15 Physical disabilities and mental illness can also arouse prejudice and discrimination. Despite the protection of the law, disabled people still encounter discrimination, some of which is more 'active' than the lack of provision of special facilities for them. For example, a disabled person may find it hard to get a job because an employer is unjustly nervous about taking on a 'risky' member of staff.

 ## REVISION QUESTIONS

1 Define prejudice and discrimination.

2 From whom do we get our prejudices?

3 Define racism, sexism and homophobia.

4 What evidence is there for a decline in homophobia in society?

GOING DEEPER

5 Is resistance to the ordination of women sexist? Give reasons for and against in your answer.

6 Why do many Christian Churches prevent practising homosexuals from being ministers/priests?

7 What signs are there of society making provision for the physically disabled?

TOPIC 6

War and peace

Stories

Following the terrorist attacks on September 11, 2001 (which killed nearly 3,000 people), there was a military campaign in Afghanistan intended to capture or kill the terrorists and overthrow the Taliban regime, which had offered refuge and support to the terrorists. Much of the fighting took place where many civilians lived. There have been over 3,000 Afghan casualties.

On one occasion a platoon of soldiers believed that they had cornered a group of terrorists in some caves. They proposed using gas to kill them or flush them out. An army chaplain was there and advised that there might only be civilians hiding there, in which case they would be contravening the Geneva Convention's rules about the treatment of civilians. (For more on the Geneva Convention, see page 75.) The commander followed the chaplain's advice. Shortly afterwards, only an old man and some children emerged from the caves.

A plane hits one of the Twin Towers of the World Trade Center, New York, September 11, 2001

Copyright © Press Association

During the 1950s, white people controlled the government of South Africa although they were in the minority. They imposed a policy of apartheid to keep white and other ethnic groups apart. This situation led to the formation of the African National Congress (ANC), which sought change by non-violent means.

On one famous occasion in 1960, between 5,000 and 7,000 people gathered at Sharpeville police station to protest against the pass laws. These laws restricted the movement of non-whites in areas of the country reserved for white people. The apartheid government's police fired at the crowd indiscriminately, killing 69 people and injuring 180.

This attack provoked the ANC into pursuing their objectives through armed struggle. Nelson Mandela and other leaders of the ANC were imprisoned. Thirty years later, Nelson Mandela was freed and subsequently elected as the first black President of a non-apartheid South Africa, which has since achieved substantial success economically and in racial integration.

By 1944, Germany was losing the Second World War against the Allies. However, there seemed little prospect of an early end to the conflict while Hitler remained in power. Some of the Germans opposed to Hitler proposed assassination as a means of hastening the end of the war (in the hope that a change of leadership might lead to surrender). Others, among them Helmuth von Moltke, believed that the use of force could never be justified. In July of that year, Claus von Stauffenberg successfully left a bomb that exploded at a meeting Hitler was attending. Although others were killed, Hitler survived and brutally executed those implicated in the 'July Plot'.

Glossary

blockade the use of force to block communications to a country or region

collateral damage unintended damage that occurs alongside intended damage, e.g. wounding or killing civilians near a military target

economic sanctions economic penalties imposed by a country or countries, e.g. a ban on importing or exporting goods from certain countries

intrinsically wrong something that is wrong in itself

ius ad bellum the branch of law (*ius*) that defines conditions that must be met for a state to be justified in going to war (*ad bellum*)

ius in bello the branch of law (*ius*) that sets out what is permissible once a state is engaged in war (*in bello*)

ius post bellum the law (*ius*) governing what happens at the end of and after (*post*) a war (*bellum*), including peace treaties and the trials of war criminals

pacifism a peaceful response to aggression (from the Latin word *pax*, meaning 'peace'). Absolute pacifists are always against war; qualified pacifists allow it in some circumstances

realism seeing war as a 'realistic' political choice not concerned with morality

smart weapons those that can be guided precisely, limiting collateral damage

 Discussion

Look at the stories again:

- If you had been the commander in Afghanistan, what would you have done?
- Does the number of deaths in the Twin Towers attack justify causing as many casualties in Afghanistan?
- Were the ANC justified in switching from a non-violent response to an armed one?
- In war time, is it right to try to assassinate a leader in the hope of ending the war and limiting the number of further casualties?

 INTRODUCTION AND MAIN POINTS

The world is always at war. Since the end of the Second World War in 1945, there has never been a day when conflict has not affected some part of the world. Our newspapers and TV screens are continually filled with war coverage. Although people's reactions and attitudes to war vary, few, if any, would want to live in a country affected by war. Those who have experienced war know that it is preferable to live in peacetime conditions.

The main ethical questions posed by war are:

- whether to fight;
- when to fight;
- how to fight.

The principal responses to these questions are:

1 **pacifism**, which assumes that the use of force is essentially wrong and rejects war as an option in all or most cases;

2 *Just War theory*, which prescribes conditions that have to be met for a war to be 'just' or 'justified' in Christian terms;

3 *realism*, which argues that waging war is a matter of 'realistic' political choice and not morality.

Celebrating the end of the Second World War in Europe: VE Day in the East End of London, 1945

Pacifism and Just War theory are specifically Christian responses. Jesus himself could readily have been classed as a pacifist. He called the peacemakers blessed, told his disciples not to respond to violence with violence ('turn the other cheek', see Matthew 5.39), rebuked those who would have used force when he was arrested ('all who take the sword will perish by the sword', Matthew 26.52) and forgave his enemies as he was dying on the cross.

Jesus' rejection of violence was the principal reason that, for the first few centuries, Christians were opposed to the use of force. The end of the Roman Empire and the experience of conflict in North Africa led St Augustine to find a way of justifying the use of force by Christians in exceptional circumstances. This move began what is called the Just War tradition – it might be better called the 'justified war' tradition; the one which identifies when we are justified in using force.

Lt Colonel Tim Collins, before battle began in Iraq in 2003, addressed his men in these terms, frequently referring to the need to behave properly in war:

> We go to liberate, not to conquer. We will not fly our flags in their country. We are entering Iraq to free a people and the only flag which will be flown in that ancient land is their own. Show respect for them . . .
>
> But if you are ferocious in battle, remember to be magnanimous in victory . . .
>
> It is a big step to take another human life. It is not to be done lightly. I know of men who have taken life needlessly in other conflicts. I can assure you they live with the mark of Cain upon them. If someone surrenders to you then remember they have that right in international law, and ensure that one day they go home to their family . . .
>
> If you harm the regiment or its history by over-enthusiasm in killing or in cowardice, know it is your family who will suffer. You will be shunned unless your conduct is of the highest, for your deeds will follow you down through history. We will bring shame on neither our uniform nor our nation.

(http://news.bbc.co.uk/1/hi/uk/2866581.stm)

Pacifism

Those who opt for a peaceful response to aggression are called pacifists, from the Latin word *pax*, meaning 'peace'. Some are always against war – absolute pacifists – and others are against war in most circumstances – qualified pacifists.

Absolute pacifists

Absolute pacifists reject war in all circumstances. They regard war and its taking of human life as being in absolute conflict with the duty to respect human life as sacred.

The absolute pacifist approach effectively outlaws war. This might be a good thing in an ideal world but it could lead to nations being unable to defend themselves if attacked.

Qualified pacifists

Qualified pacifists are very unwilling to consider war an option, believing that the benefits of war rarely, if ever, justify engaging in it. Since war leads to so much suffering, qualified pacifists take some convincing that a war will be 'worth it'.

However, they recognize that being prepared to believe that a war is 'worth it' means accepting that innocent people will die. After all, no weapons can be so 'smart' that innocent people are never hurt or killed. There is also the problem of not being able to foresee accurately what will happen in a war. For example, some believed that the four-year-long First World War (1914–18) would be over in weeks.

Lord Soper (1903–98), a Methodist campaigner for peace, at Speakers' Corner, Hyde Park

Conscientious objection

Pacifists who will not fight may, if their country's law permits it, register as conscientious objectors. This exemption can make those who do fight resentful (one way in which people showed their anger towards conscientious objectors during the First World War was to send them white feathers, which symbolized cowardice).

Quakers have always taken a pacifist line and were among those who campaigned for the principle of conscientious objection in the UK (adopted in 1916). The Roman Catholic Church expects conscientious objectors to volunteer for other duties apart from fighting (ambulance work, etc.).

Bertrand Russell (Earl Russell, 1872–1970), a British academic, was a conscientious objector who went to prison for his beliefs during the First World War, but he supported the Second World War

Non-violence

Many pacifists suggest non-violent resistance to aggression as an alternative to war. They cite Mahatma Gandhi's non-violent campaign against British rule in India and Martin Luther King's campaign for the civil rights of African Americans (see page 62). Their critics argue that while these campaigns influenced events, there is no instance when non-violent resistance has of itself succeeded. For example, Gandhi influenced public opinion, but it was exhaustion from fighting the Second World War that led to Britain's withdrawal from India and other colonies. Moreover, had ruthless regimes like Hitler's been met with 'peaceful opposition', the opposition would have simply been crushed.

Gandhi and the Salt March: non-violent protest

The British government in India – before India achieved independence – imposed a salt tax, which gave the government a monopoly on the production and sale of salt. As part of his campaign for Indian independence from British rule, Gandhi decided on a non-violent protest against this monopoly.

His choosing the salt tax for his protest had mass appeal because everyone, from aristocrat to peasant, understood the need for salt: all people have to consume it to replace the salt lost through sweating, especially in a hot climate like India's.

Gandhi led a march to the coastal village of Dandi, on the Arabian Sea, where salt could easily be found. He set out on 12 March 1930, accompanied by 78 male companions. By the time they reached the coast, others had joined them, forming a great procession stretching at least two miles in length. On 6 April, Gandhi picked up a lump of mud and salt and boiled it in sea water to produce the commodity that no Indian was allowed to make.

He encouraged his supporters to follow his example and make salt. Salt came to be sold illegally all over the coast of India. The British responded by imprisoning over 60,000 people, including Gandhi himself.

However, Gandhi's actions had attracted worldwide attention and convinced many, both inside and outside India, of the rightness of the campaign for independence. Moreover, when he was released the following year, Gandhi began negotiations with Lord Irwin, the Viceroy of India, and they reached an agreement, the Gandhi–Irwin Pact. This pact did not bring about independence (which was ultimately conceded only in 1947 by a British government exhausted by the Second World War) but the language of the agreement marked an important step towards independence. The pact used phrases such as 'it is agreed', which indicated that the British had been negotiating and were no longer simply giving orders; it also demonstrated to the world the power of non-violent protest.

Mahatma Gandhi (1869–1948) formulated and led non-violent resistance to British rule in India

Just War

The Just War theory has a long history. Its origins lie about 1,600 years ago when St Augustine (AD 354–430) first established the conditions under which Christians might justify the use of force. This question had become urgent because the Roman Empire was threatened by invasion in the fifth century and Christianity had become its official religion during the previous century.

Strictly, there are three aspects to Just War theory (their Latin shorthand names are given in brackets):

1 When is a state justified in going to war? (*Ius ad bellum*)

2 How should a state behave in war? (*Ius in bello*)

3 How should a state make peace after a war? (*Ius post bellum*)

When is a state justified in going to war? (*Ius ad bellum*)

Just cause

A country that is invaded, or believes that it will be invaded, by an aggressor has 'cause' to defend itself to protect human and political rights. Its citizens could have their human rights threatened in many ways, e.g. the prospect of losing their homes, the closure of schools and the suppression of free speech. Their political rights could be threatened by their loss of the right to vote or govern themselves.

Sometimes, a country is too small or too weak to defend itself. In this case, Just War theory allows one nation to assist another in defending itself.

There are also occasions when one country has good reason to believe that another is building up weapons and forces to attack it. The country arming for war might try to drag out diplomatic negotiations to give it more time to strengthen its forces. Hitler used this tactic in the period before the Second World War.

Just War theory allows a state that believes it might be attacked to attack the potential aggressor first – a pre-emptive action called 'anticipatory self-defence'. With an advance strike, the potential victim has a greater likelihood of succeeding against the aggressor than if it waits until the aggressor attacks. The reason such behaviour might be morally acceptable is that, in theory, peace would be restored relatively quickly, resulting in less suffering. However, this argument has to be carefully balanced with the idea of using force only as a last resort (see page 73).

Right intention

St Augustine, the originator of Just War theory, condemned revenge as a motive for going to war. This view means, for instance, that a powerful country cannot justify attacking another simply because it disapproves of that country's behaviour, e.g. over human rights. It must also intend to right the wrong.

Therefore 'just cause' has to be linked to 'right intention' or 'good motive'. There must be no hidden (ulterior) motives, e.g. a country would lack 'right intention' if its stated objective was to right an abuse of human rights but its actual intention was to gain access to an important natural resource, such as oil.

Lawful authority exercised lawfully

If *any* person or group within a society could declare war, law and order would break down. Such a breakdown occurs in circumstances of civil war or when terrorist acts are committed.

When St Thomas Aquinas (*c.* 1225–74) was developing the theory of Just War, he wanted to guard against warlords or barons having the right to declare war. From his point of view, only a sovereign – a king or prince – could decide to go to war. This interpretation of Just War theory means that, in a modern democracy, only the duly elected leaders may declare war and they must follow a public, legal process when they do so.

However, there are many societies that are undemocratic and are governed oppressively. In these nations, opposition might arise and resort to military force. Whether they have 'lawful authority' will be hotly disputed. On the one hand, those seeking greater freedom ('freedom fighters') will argue that their voice cannot be heard and that the behaviour of an oppressive government deprives that government of 'lawful authority'. On the other, the oppressive regime might portray its enemies as 'terrorists'.

Last resort

Since war is an evil to be avoided, it must only be undertaken when all other means have been tried and exhausted.

Following the Second World War and the establishment of the United Nations (UN), the member states of the UN formulated an internationally recognized range of measures that could be used as alternatives to war. The measures include diplomacy, **economic sanctions** and **blockades**. Usually, the severity of these measures is stepped up only if the least aggressive ones fail. However, sometimes it is argued that the early use of 'strong' measures would be more effective. One reason is that 'gentle' measures, like economic sanctions, can cause just as much suffering to the poorest and weakest in society as a war. The rulers of the countries against which sanctions are imposed tend to get what they need, while the poor and, in particular, children do not. For example, after the war in 1990, Iraq was almost reduced to a pre-industrial state by sanctions and was unable to rebuild its infrastructure. Children died (estimates vary from 670,000 to 880,000) because they lacked the kind of medical care that they would have received before sanctions were imposed.

There are, therefore, occasions on which a war is fought because it is regarded as the 'lesser of two evils', i.e. that, although war will bring about suffering and loss of life, there will be less suffering than if no war had been fought.

The United Nations building (*left*) and inside the United Nations Security Council (*right*)

Realistic chance of success

No state should undertake a war without a realistic chance of success.

If a small state were to attack a much larger one (with just cause and right intention, etc.), the outcome of war is unlikely to be the 'lesser of two evils'. Rather, it is likely that a greater degree of suffering would ensue because the smaller state would probably be heavily defeated by the larger power. To give an absurd example, there would be little point in Luxembourg, a tiny European state, declaring war against France, which is much more powerful.

Proportionality

Proportionality refers to the need for a state – before it goes to war – to consider the proportion of *universal* good that might ensue from going to war (e.g. achieving the just cause) in relation to the *universal* evils (casualties, especially). 'Universal' has to be stressed because often a state will estimate only the costs and benefits to itself and ignore the costs and benefits experienced by the enemy and any innocent third parties.

There is a substantial element of guesswork in making such judgements. Important factors to consider include:

- how effective the use of '**smart weapons**' will be (i.e. whether a technologically superior power can disable a less sophisticated enemy by disrupting communications and defence systems, and causing only a minimal number of casualties);
- whether the enemy forces will offer much resistance;
- whether an unscrupulous enemy will try to use civilians to 'shield' the armed forces.

How should a state behave in war? (*Ius in bello*)

In the *ius ad bellum* section, we examined the conditions necessary for a state to begin a war. However, its moral obligations do not end there. How military forces behave *in war* – however justified they might be in going to war – also counts. A state has to ensure that its military forces continue to act according to moral principles in war, i.e. *ius in bello* conditions have to be applied.

There are three basic *ius in bello* conditions: discrimination, proportionality and that weapons or methods evil in themselves cannot be used.

Discrimination

Military forces can wage war only against those 'engaged in harm', which means that they cannot attack civilians. Modern 'smart' technology makes such discrimination easier but it is, in practice, difficult to avoid **collateral damage** (polite or evasive jargon for civilian casualties). Sometimes, unscrupulous leaders will try to station their forces among the civilian population or even dress their forces as civilians to exploit this condition.

Proportionality

Proportionality in this context means that the amount of force used should be in proportion to the severity of the threat – in other words, it prohibits 'overkill'. This idea means, for example, that the use of tactical (let alone large) nuclear weapons, or chemical or biological warfare, is unlikely ever to be regarded as proportionate because their impact is too great. (You could also argue that the impact of such weapons is very difficult to calculate and that, therefore, you could never accurately measure it in proportion to any benefit.)

Weapons or methods evil in themselves (mala in se) cannot be used

This condition overlaps with the other two *ius in bello* conditions. Certain methods are **intrinsically wrong** and so cannot be used in war. Mass rape campaigns, genocide or ethnic cleansing, torturing captured enemy soldiers and using weapons with uncontrollable effects, e.g. those that are chemical or biological, are all considered to be evil in themselves.

Nuclear warfare

It is often argued that some weapons are so destructive that they make Just War theory irrelevant. This belief is particularly true of nuclear weapons, which their critics claim could never be used proportionally.

Two atomic bombs were dropped on Hiroshima and Nagasaki, Japan, in August 1945. During the following 45 years, the USA and the former Soviet Union amassed vast numbers of nuclear weapons and were engaged in what was called the Cold War ('cold' since the weapons were never used; a 'hot' war involves using weapons and killing people).

The principal reason neither side used the weapons was that there was a 'balance of terror' or 'mutually assured destruction' (known,

appropriately, as MAD). This build-up of weapons made many fear for the very survival of humanity and our planet – the view taken by Pope John XXIII in *Pacem in Terris* (see page 77). Activist groups were set up and, in the

Copyright © Shutterstock

Ground Zero, Hiroshima, the site of the first atomic bomb dropped on Japan in 1945

UK, included CND (the Campaign for Nuclear Disarmament).

Some argued that the only way to steer the nations away from this danger was for those who possessed weapons to voluntarily give them up. This disarmament might be done by one nation at a time (unilateral disarmament) or by several nations acting together (multilateral disarmament). Treaties limiting and reducing stockpiles of weapons were agreed.

Anxiety in the twenty-first century focuses on the risk of nuclear weapons falling into the hands of terrorists and on the possibility of states unfriendly to the West acquiring them. A treaty exists to prevent the spread of nuclear weapons; it is called the Nuclear Non-Proliferation Treaty (NNPT).

How should a state make peace after war? (*Ius post bellum*)

Most writing about Just War focuses on the conditions that have to be met before a Christian can accept that going to war is 'just' or the 'lesser of two evils'. However, as we have seen, Just War theory is also concerned with the way in which a war is fought, i.e. that civilian casualties are prevented and that prisoners are treated humanely. These approaches shaped the Geneva Convention.

The Geneva Convention refers to the treaty of 1949, which defines the basic rights of people captured during military conflicts, protection for those wounded in war, and protection for those in and around a conflict zone. The 1949 treaty followed on from the Nuremburg War Trials of Nazi war criminals. The first Geneva Convention was agreed in 1864, following Henri Dunant's book, *Memoir of Solferino*, on the horrors of war. There were further Conventions in 1906 and 1929.

The Geneva Conventions remain the foundation of contemporary international humanitarian law: they have been applied during the Iraq War (2003), the Afghan War (2001 – present) and the war in Georgia (2008).

In a sense, defeating an enemy is only the start of winning a war. If a victorious army withdraws from a defeated nation leaving chaos, it might undermine the very reasons for which it went to war. For example, the victorious nation state might have warred against the defeated state because the latter had an oppressive regime that ruled without regard to human rights. It would therefore make sense for the victorious state to ensure that human rights were restored in the defeated nation. If those rights were not restored, then one of the main aims for fighting would not be achieved. This understanding was the principal reason for the Marshall Plan which made a vast amount of money available for the reconstruction of Europe after the Second World War. This stage of the Just War is called *ius post bellum* (justice after war).

Conditions for a just peace
Just as there are conditions for waging a Just War, there are conditions for a just peace.

1 *Just cause for termination*. A state may terminate a war if the human rights that had been violated can be restored and the aggressor is willing to agree to terms of surrender, i.e. to make compensations, agree to holding war crimes trials and make a formal apology. Alternatively, a state may terminate a war if the just goals of the war cannot be achieved or if achieving them would entail the use of excessive force.

2 *Right intention*. The victor must not pursue revenge and, in investigating war crimes, it must give attention to those committed by its own side.

3 *Discrimination*. A distinction must be drawn between politicians, armed forces and civilians. Civilian populations must not be made to suffer for the decisions made by their leaders or for atrocities committed by soldiers.

4 *Proportionality*. In keeping with the previous conditions, the victor is forbidden from treating the defeated nation and its people disproportionately. That is, the victor should not enforce humiliating terms of surrender or treat the defeated people with less respect than anyone else.

Since war is defensible only in limited circumstances, the basis of just peacemaking is to restore 'normality' as soon as possible.

Realism

When discussing war ethics, some people claim that they are 'realists'. They see international affairs as a 'jungle' in which only power counts and moral considerations are a handicap.

Realists point to the fact that warfare is a constant in human history. For example, since the end of the Second World War in 1945, there has not been a single day when there has not been war in some part of the world.

Realists argue that, because the effects of war are so awful, a democratic state should avoid being involved in war for anything other than national self-interest. It should also ensure that it can win.

There are two kinds of realism: descriptive and prescriptive.

Descriptive realism

Descriptive realism claims that observing the behaviour of nation states reveals that they are driven by self-interest, not morality. Self-interest might result from the competition that exists between states for power and resources. Alternatively, those who rule might make a conscious choice to be self-interested. For the sake of self-interest and self-preservation, a state might choose to go to war and to ignore moral considerations (such as Just War conditions), if those considerations get in the way of victory.

However, critics of descriptive realism argue that a state is made up of individuals for whom morality matters. Eventually, their sense of outrage might oblige their leaders to take morality into consideration. Also, states do not usually decide to go to war on impulse. Debate, including the application of moral principles, often precedes the decision to fight.

Prescriptive realism

Since the world is a 'jungle' where the strongest survive, it is prudent for a state not to be hampered by moral considerations in international politics. Significantly, this approach normally includes some rules, like 'wars should only be fought in self-defence'. These rules might appear to be similar to the Just War ones, but they are not based on arguments about what is 'right' or 'just' but on what is 'practical' or 'prudent'.

GOING DEEPER

The Bible

There is considerable diversity in the Old Testament. The sixth of the Ten Commandments forbids the taking of life – 'You shall not murder' (Exodus 20.13) – but, in contrast, there are many Old Testament stories describing God as fighting for his nation Israel and commanding followers to fight. If a wrong was committed, the Israelites were to take 'life for life, eye for eye, tooth for tooth, hand for hand, foot for foot' (Exodus 21.23–24). On the other hand, one of the last books of the Old Testament, Micah, has a vision of a time when weapons of war will be turned into agricultural tools: 'they shall beat their swords into ploughshares' (Micah 4.3).

Jesus' teaching and example are emphatically on the side of peace and the avoidance of violence. He taught: 'Blessed are the peacemakers for they will be called children of God' (Matthew 5.9). He also seems to reverse the Old Testament teaching of an 'eye for an eye': 'You have heard that it was said, "An eye for an eye and a tooth for a tooth." But I say to you, Do not resist an evildoer. But if anyone strikes you on the right cheek, turn the other also' (Matthew 5.38–39).

Jesus also gave his disciples the example of non-resistance in the face of violent injustice. He did not resist his arrest and, while he was dying on the cross, forgave his enemies.

Roman Catholic Church

Arguably the most important Christian document about war and peace in the past half century is the encyclical (see page 26) that Pope John XXIII published in 1963, entitled *Peace on Earth* (or *Pacem in Terris*, its Latin name). Usually, such encyclicals are meant for the bishops and clergy of the Church. But the Pope aimed this encyclical at a much wider readership because the fear of nuclear warfare dominated international attention at that time.

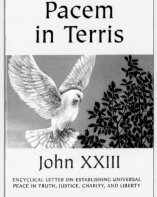

Pope John taught that:

> Men nowadays are becoming more and more convinced that any disputes which may arise between nations must be resolved by negotiation and agreement, and not by recourse to arms. We acknowledge that this conviction owes its origin chiefly to the terrifying destructive force of modern weapons.
> (John XXIII, *Pacem in Terris*)

Church of England

There are many Church of England documents about when war might be considered an option. The advice that the House of Bishops (a meeting of all the bishops who jointly issue teaching) gave before the 2003 Iraq War shows how much the Church of England relies upon the Just War tradition. The bishops said that they used the approach associated with the Just War tradition because:

> Despite its limitations, just war thinking seeks to establish the principles, criteria and rules that can help Christians to make a judgement

The Ten Commandments

as to whether a particular use of force is morally acceptable or even desirable. Its utility has been shaped and sustained through an ongoing dialogue between Christian and secular authorities over many centuries.

(House of Bishops, *Evaluating the Threat of Military Action against Iraq*)

Society of Friends (Quakers)

The Quakers do not have a set of authoritative beliefs (unlike the Roman Catholic Church, which has its Catechism). They prefer to talk about giving testimony. Their most famous is the so-called Peace Testimony, which they adopted in the seventeenth century. This statement points to Jesus' example of non-violence and tries to imitate it: 'We are a people that follow after those things that make for peace, love and unity; it is our desire that others' feet may walk in the same' (Margaret Fell, 1660; see www.qfp.quakerweb.org.uk/qfp19-46.html).

Peace

The day on which the First World War ended was 11 November 1918. On 8 May 1945, German forces surrendered unconditionally on all fronts, ending the Second World War in Europe. However, neither day brought peace in the sense that people living in the prosperous democracies of Western Europe understand peace today. At the end of each World War, there were many refugees who had no homes or jobs.

Types of 'peace'

So, peace is more than the end of war. In the Old Testament, peace is depicted as a time when weapons of war will be melted down and cast into the tools of agriculture (Micah 4.3), which in turn will feed people and create prosperity. The prophet Micah believed that such a situation could only be brought about by God and by human beings obeying his will. This kind of peace can be given the shorthand name *shalom*, the Hebrew word for 'peace'.

Shalom is a different kind of peace from 'keeping the peace', which is the kind secured by military power. In Jesus' time, the Romans

The train carriage where the First World War Armistice was signed in 1918, and some of the people who signed the truce

used their legions to suppress conflict and keep order. This imposed peace was called the *Pax Romana* (from Latin *pax*, translated as 'peace'). *Pax* can be used as a shorthand term for an enforced 'peace', in which law and order are maintained through the threat of violence.

Such a peace was enforced by the British throughout their empire in the nineteenth century. This peace is sometimes called the *Pax Britannica*. The USA, as the only remaining superpower, is frequently involved in the same kind of 'peace keeping', *Pax Americana*, in the twenty-first century.

The two kinds of peace – *pax* and *shalom* – are not unrelated. Without law and order, it is difficult to build the kind of society that the Old Testament prophets looked forward to. However, for *shalom* to grow out of *pax*, people need to work together. They have to believe that the resources and services in society are fairly distributed among them. They have to think that there is justice. That is why the Christian churches often teach about peace and justice together.

⦿ SUMMARY

1 War occurs when states resort to the use of force to resolve disagreements. Christians have often asserted that the conditions of Just War theory must be met to justify such action.

2 Some Christians, pacifists, insist that war is never or rarely a Christian option. Christians also have a concept of peace that goes beyond simply the point when conflict ends.

3 Pacifists prefer peace to war. Some are against war in any circumstances – absolute pacifists. Others reject war in most circumstances – qualified pacifists.

4 The problems with qualified pacifism are that assessing whether a war will be 'worth it' is difficult and rests on the assumption that the death of innocent people can be justified (inevitably some of the dead will not be soldiers, however well focused the use of force might be).

5 Non-violence has been supported by many important leaders, e.g. Gandhi and Martin Luther King. However, there is no evidence that it works on its own. Also, ruthless governments like Hitler's would simply stamp on peaceful opposition.

6 War has afflicted the world continuously since the end of the Second World War.

7 The principal ethical questions are whether, when and how to fight.

8 The principal answers to these questions are Just War, realism and pacifism.

9 Just War theory is 1,600 years old. St Augustine was the first to formulate it and St Thomas Aquinas had a profound effect on the way it is now understood.

10 Just War theory is probably the most influential of the three main approaches (Just War, realism and pacifism) and can be considered under three headings:

  (a) when it is just to fight a war (*ius ad bellum*);

  (b) how to behave in war (*ius in bello*);

  (c) what to do after a war (*ius post bellum*).

11 When to fight has the following conditions (listed with examples):

  (a) just cause: human rights abused, another country is amassing arms with the intention of attacking your state;

  (b) right intention: never from revenge, always to right an obvious 'wrong';

  (c) lawful authority: governments (especially elected ones) have the authority to fight other states, terrorists do not;

  (d) last resort: other methods, especially diplomacy, must have failed before force is used;

  (e) realistic chance of success: since war is the 'lesser of two evils' and is, therefore, intended to cause less harm than doing nothing, a nation should not go to war if it is likely to fail as this would lead to more suffering rather than less;

  (f) proportionality: there has to be a 'cost-benefit analysis'; the gains of war must exceed their likely cost in human life (this is very difficult to assess).

12 A state should behave in war with:

  (a) discrimination: force should be used against military personnel, not civilians;

  (b) proportionality: only 'enough' force should be used, tactical use of nuclear, chemical or biological weapons is ruled out;

  (c) knowledge that certain weapons and methods are evil in themselves: for example, mass rape, ethnic cleansing, torture, and biological and chemical weapons because they have incalculable, therefore disproportionate, effects.

13 To truly win a war, the original objectives for going to war must have been met, e.g. the restoration of human rights. There are 'conditions for peace':

(a) just cause for termination: a state may terminate a war once violated human rights are restored and surrender terms agreed, or if just goals cannot be achieved or would be achieved only with excessive force;

(b) right intention: the victor must not pursue revenge;

(c) discrimination: civilians must be treated differently from their leaders or those who committed atrocities;

(d) proportionality: the defeated must not be humiliated.

14 Realists see international affairs as a jungle where the strongest survive and moral considerations will only handicap governments. There are two kinds of realism:

(a) Descriptive realism: an approach that arises from observing (or 'describing') the behaviour of nation states and reaching the conclusion that morality does not affect their behaviour. (However, critics of descriptive realism point out that the opinions of a state's populace might ultimately affect its leaders' conduct.)

(b) Prescriptive realism: an approach that arises from the belief that, to survive, you must do ('prescribe') what is 'practical' or 'prudent' rather than what is 'just' or 'moral'.

GOING DEEPER

15 The Bible includes a range of attitudes to war. There is support for revenge ('an eye for an eye') but also the vision of peace, where weapons become agricultural tools. Jesus provides the supreme example of non-violence: he does not resist arrest and forgives his persecutors as he dies on the cross.

 REVISION QUESTIONS

1 What is the difference between an absolute pacifist and a qualified pacifist?

2 Give the three Latin phrases that describe the main aspects of Just War theory.

3 List the six conditions required for a war to be classified as 'just'.

4 Name two leaders who have supported non-violent protest. Give an example of what form non-violent protest might take.

5 What is meant by discrimination?

6 What is meant by proportionality?

7 What is the difference between descriptive realism and prescriptive realism?

GOING DEEPER

8 Give the name of a biblical text that appears to support revenge.

9 Which is the supreme example of non-violence in the Bible?

Wealth and poverty

Stories

Poverty is not something that belongs in the past or simply to remote countries. Victorian Britain knew terrible extremes of poverty and some persists today. There are parts of the developing world that are poorer than anything ever experienced in the UK.

Victorian Manchester

In Victorian Manchester, wealth was concentrated in the hands of a very small number of residents. These rich Mancunians lived longer and vastly more comfortably than the working people who produced the wealth but lived in terrible poverty. Innumerable reports from the time record a story of poor wages, excessive working hours, dangerous working conditions, unsanitary accommodation, an absence of health care, high infant mortality and a short **life expectancy**. Children, in particular, because they were paid far less than adults, were cruelly exploited. For example, in the cotton mills, the youngest children were employed to crawl beneath machinery (while it was still in operation) to gather up loose cotton; many died by getting caught up in the machinery.

Modern Britain

At the end of the nineteenth century, Seebohm Rowntree defined poverty as not being able to afford a 'shopping basket of food, housing and items of clothing'. By the 1950s, such a definition was outdated, as most people had these items (there was close to full employment and the welfare state supported those out of work and provided social housing). According to the Rowntree Foundation (founded by Seebohm Rowntree's father Joseph to investigate the causes of social problems) key tell-tale signs of poverty in modern Britain include:

- not having a high-street bank account;
- having to spend more than 10 per cent of any income on energy bills;
- poor access to transport, employment opportunities or healthy food.

The Rowntree Foundation estimates that roughly 20 per cent of the population suffers deprivation, while a hardcore of two to three million are in deep poverty, a plight which would be recognizable to Seebohm Rowntree.

(http://news.bbc.co.uk/1/hi/business/4070112.stm)

The world's 'least liveable country'

The United Nations names Sierra Leone as the world's 'least liveable' country, based on its poverty and the poor quality of life that its citizens must endure. In 2004, Sierra Leone imported far more than it exported; it had only 52 miles (84 kilometres) of railway and only about 8 per cent of its roads were paved.

We can get some perspective on Sierra Leone's economic misery by comparing its GNP (gross national product) per capita (the income that each person would have annually if GNP were divided equally) with that of the world's richest countries. Sierra Leone's GNP per capita of about $550 is 72 times less than Americans enjoy.

(http://internationaltrade.suite101.com/)

Glossary

free trade ensuring that there are no tariffs or barriers to the free exchange of goods and services

General Synod an assembly, sometimes called the Church of England's parliament, which brings together bishops, clergy and lay people

Global South the countries of the world – mainly in the southern hemisphere – that have medium or low human development

justice the quality of being fair and unbiased, to do what is right

life expectancy the average number of years that someone can expect to live, e.g. someone born in the poorest country in the world might expect to live just 32 years, whereas someone from the richest might expect to live for over 80 years

literacy the ability to read and write (a significant factor because there is a strong connection between literacy and prosperity; countries with lower literacy rates tend to be poorer)

materialistic describes a lifestyle in which the pursuit of wealth and luxury – materialism – is the main priority

stewardship taking responsibility for something that belongs to someone else, e.g. in Christian and Jewish thought, human beings are stewards of the earth, which ultimately belongs to God

trade justice ensuring that trade is conducted on a just basis, i.e. without wealthy nations or international companies exploiting weaker and poorer people

Discussion

- The Inland Revenue says that 21 per cent of UK wealth is owned by 1 per cent of the population. Do you think this is fair?

INTRODUCTION AND MAIN POINTS

In the nineteenth century, many people moved from the countryside to work in cities such as Birmingham, Manchester, Leeds and Bradford. The living conditions for many were terrible, with poor hygiene, diet and health, and short life expectancy. It took the social reforms of the twentieth century, especially the creation of the Welfare State after the Second World War, to change this situation.

Today, everyone has access to state support if they are out of work or on a low income, and everyone has access to free health care and education. All these measures are paid for from taxes.

However, there remain many people – although fewer than in the nineteenth century – who still live in poor housing, have poor employment prospects, poor health and lower life expectancy. Eradicating poverty is

less easy than the social reformers of the twentieth century hoped.

Poverty in our own country remains the concern of successive governments. However, poverty in other countries also concerns many people, which is why campaigns such as Live Aid, Band Aid, Make Poverty History and Children in Need attract such attention.

What is poverty?

'Poverty is hunger. Poverty is lack of shelter. Poverty is being sick and not being able to see a doctor. Poverty is not having access to school and not knowing how to read. Poverty is not having a job, is fear for the future, living one day at a time. Poverty is losing a child to illness brought about by unclean water. Poverty is powerlessness, lack of representation and freedom.'

(www.fightpoverty.mmbrico.com/poverty/what.html)

Aid

There are different kinds of aid:

- *Emergency aid*: when a disaster occurs, it is necessary to respond to the emergency immediately.

- *Long-term aid*: most charities are concerned not only to offer emergency help, but also to assist people to become self-reliant. Aid workers set up partnerships with local groups to empower people to improve their own situations.

- *Speaking out/prophetic aid*: many problems, however, are not going to be sorted out by emergency aid or by helping people to be self-reliant. The difficulties are the result of fundamental political and economic injustices that require political or economic action. The abolition of slavery in the early nineteenth century is a good example. It was only after relentless campaigning by William Wilberforce and his supporters that slavery was abolished in the British Empire. Ultimately, it required an Act of Parliament. In the same way, the relief of debt in the developing world, the relief of poverty and ending the HIV & AIDS pandemic are dependent upon international political and economic action.

THE CHRISTIAN ATTITUDE TO WEALTH

Concern for the poor has Christian roots. It is at the heart of Christian thinking and many of the social reformers in our history were driven by their Christian beliefs.

Concern for the poor is at the heart of Jesus' teaching. He said more about the poor and the use of wealth than he did about other moral questions.

How should Christians use money?

Many Christians, inspired by Jesus' teaching, have devoted their lives to relieving poverty and suffering. Some have even given up their personal property to live in monastic communities.

On the other hand, British society is **materialistic**: we live in a society where many are driven by the desire to make money, spend it and acquire things.

This lifestyle can seem a long way from Jesus' teaching. He told people to give away their possessions and he warned those who followed him to expect no material security (Jesus said, 'Foxes have holes, and

birds of the air have nests; but the Son of Man has nowhere to lay his head' (Luke 9.58)).

God's ownership of the earth

At first sight, this teaching can seem odd or 'crazy' to modern people living in a rich Western country. To understand it better, we need to know a bit about the Jewish culture which Jesus came from. The Jews believed that God 'owned' the earth – he originally had 'dominion' over the earth and

God says in the first creation story in Genesis: 'Have dominion over the fish of the sea, and over the birds of the air . . . and over every creeping thing that creeps upon the earth' (Genesis 1.26).

handed it to human beings – and that human beings were temporary tenants or stewards of the earth.

We can understand this view quite easily: we didn't shape the environment we are born into. Eventually, we die and we leave what we have done to the environment behind us. Therefore environmentalists constantly remind us of the effect our behaviour has on the earth. They are concerned that we could leave behind a planet so badly affected by global warming that life could become impossible in some places.

In the story told by Jesus, the rich man and Lazarus found themselves in very different places in the next life

Humanity's stewardship of the earth

The way in which human beings carry out their **stewardship** of the earth features widely in Jewish Scripture. The Jews were taught that they should have concern for the poor and the foreigner in their midst. For example, when they were harvesting corn, they were meant to leave something at the edge of their fields for the poor. Also, the Jewish prophets constantly criticized the rich who ignored the poor and praised those who were considerate towards them.

Jesus belongs to this tradition. In the parable of the rich man and Lazarus, the rich man is condemned for ignoring the plight of Lazarus, who is poor (Luke 16.19–31). Those who ignore the hungry, the thirsty, those in prison, etc. will be judged (see the parable of the sheep and goats, Matthew 25.31–46), while the man who helps his mugged neighbour is praised (see the parable of the good Samaritan, Luke 10.30–37).

But Jesus also commended extravagance in some circumstances (e.g. when his feet were massaged with expensive ointment), even though the poor might have been helped. So Jesus does not condemn wealth out of hand. Moreover, unless people have some wealth to share in the first place, they cannot help others. This view suggests that Christians need to establish priorities.

However, in Jesus' time there was often a concentration of wealth in the hands of the few at the expense of the poor majority. This state of affairs made it impossible for the poor to do anything to improve their situation.

Economic and social justice

Evidence of the unequal distribution and unfair use of wealth leads us to the concept of economic **justice**. Even if you give everyone the same opportunities, they will not take equal advantage of them. Some will

Moral and immoral occupations

Methodists forbid the consumption of alcohol, which means that there can be no wine at church functions. However, Church of England social occasions, such as parish picnics or church fairs, often include wine or beer. In France, every November, the Hospices de Beaune, a Roman Catholic charity, organizes a wine auction, selling the product of the 150 acres of vineyards it has owned since the sixteenth century. The proceeds benefit patients who are provided for in modern hospital buildings.

This diversity of practice over alcohol illustrates how difficult it is to generalize about whether Christians consider certain activities moral or immoral. This list of occupations (regarded by some Christians as immoral) highlights the differences:

- providing alcohol (because some people become addicted; but alcohol gives pleasure and employment to many);
- gambling (because some people become addicted; however, the industry gives employment to many);
- providing energy through nuclear power (which can be very dangerous – the Chernobyl and Fukushima nuclear power station accidents harmed many people; however, nuclear energy is cleaner than other energy sources if it is produced safely);
- making or selling military weapons (because they are used to kill or injure people, which goes against the Ten

Commandments and the teaching of Jesus; however, they might be used justly in a just war);
- scientific experiments on animals (because we have no right to treat animals in this way; however, such experimentation can result in valuable medical advances);
- working in an abortion clinic (because it is never right to take life; however, ending pregnancy might be necessary in some circumstances).

There is less disagreement among Christians over the immorality of the occupations listed here:

- those that pollute the environment (as stewards of the earth we are responsible for keeping it safe; but almost all occupations result in some degree of pollution);
- those with poor employment and human-rights records (but you could join them and work for change from within);
- those producing genetically modified (GM) foods or ones that involve embryology work (because interfering with nature goes against God's purposes; however, GM foods and advances in embryo research might lead to an improvement in some people's lives);
- the pornography industry (which exploits women; human beings are made in God's image and our bodies are temples of the Holy Spirit – see 1 Corinthians 6.19).

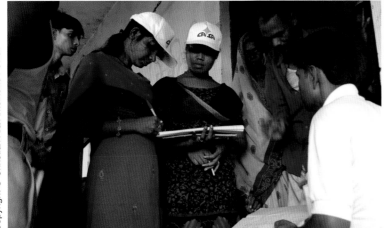

Volunteers Pampa Halder, 24, and Dipa Mandal, 20 (both wearing white caps), are responsible for a wide range of tasks within Gamaria relief camp, such as checking supplies and reading to groups of children. Here, they check a list of names of people living in the camp where a Christian Aid partner runs a feeding programme. The list is used to ensure items, including milk powder and soap, go to those who most need them. Maintaining health and personal hygiene is important in crowded relief camps. Unsanitary conditions can lead to the spread of respiratory infections and cause diarrhoea

do better than others (see the parable of the talents, Luke 19.11–27). However, it is possible for a few to dominate the market to the extent that it is almost impossible for the rest to change their situation. With regard to aid, this situation means that emergency and long-term aid are insufficient – rather, a fundamental, political change is necessary.

Fighting poverty

Many individuals make a personal contribution towards alleviating poverty, usually through a national charity. Three of the most important Christian relief and development charities in the UK are Christian Aid, Tearfund and CAFOD. While they are national charities, they work closely with similar charities from other countries. CAFOD is part of an international network of similar Roman Catholic charities.

Christian Aid

Christian Aid was set up by churches in the UK and Ireland at the end of the Second World War in 1945. It funds projects in some of the world's poorest countries and it is dedicated to helping people improve their own lives and deal with the causes of poverty and injustice. It spends more than half the donations it receives on long-term development projects; a further 11 per cent is spent on emergencies, 16 per cent on campaigning and education, 19 per cent on fundraising and 2 per cent on administration. In the overseas projects, money goes directly to local community groups and church organizations (Christian Aid's 'partners') to help people directly. The reason charities choose to work with partners arises from the belief and experience that local people know best the nature of their problems and how to solve them. Christian Aid is not political in a party-political sense but it recognizes that many of the causes of poverty, e.g. debt or unequal trade, are basically political and economic. Christian Aid helps not only Christians; its aid is given regardless of religion.

Tearfund

Tearfund is founded on the belief that Jesus responds with compassion to meet people's practical and spiritual needs. As Jesus said in John's Gospel (John 10.10): 'I came that they may have life, and have it abundantly.'

Like Christian Aid, Tearfund works through local churches and Christian agencies – Tearfund's partners – to improve prospects for the poorest people in the world. Tearfund describes its role as 'helping people become all that God wants them to be'. Support for Tearfund comes largely from Christians in the UK and Ireland; churches and individual Christians account for 83 per cent of its

income. The charity spends about 10 per cent of its money on administration and fundraising.

Tearfund has several principal areas of involvement.

- *Community development*. Communities are encouraged to plan their own initiatives, including healthcare, **literacy** classes, clean water and sanitation, HIV & AIDS education, drug rehabilitation and food security programmes.

- *Disaster response*. Tearfund offers emergency relief when flood, famine, earthquake, or war strikes communities. Tearfund also helps people who live in areas prone to natural disasters (e.g. places liable to flooding) to prevent or limit the effects such events might have.

- *Speaking out* (*being prophetic*). Tearfund tries to persuade governments to act to change people's conditions. They base this work on Proverbs 31.8: 'Speak out for those who cannot speak, for the rights of all the destitute.'

- *Helping families to be self-reliant*. For example, one way to foster self-reliance is to give small loans to groups to help them to buy land or start a business.

CAFOD

CAFOD (Catholic Agency for Overseas Development), founded in 1962, is the Roman Catholic Church in England and Wales' official overseas development and relief agency. CAFOD belongs to a worldwide network of Roman Catholic relief and development organizations, the Caritas International Federation. CAFOD spends between 85 and 90 per cent of its funds directly on its programmes to reduce global poverty and injustice.

CAFOD believes that all human beings have a right to dignity and respect, and that the world's resources are a gift to be shared equally by all men and women, whatever their race, nationality or religion.
(www.cafod.org.uk/news/protection-of-campaigners)

CAFOD raises money from the Roman Catholic community, the UK government and the general public, and is similar to Tearfund. The charity:

- promotes long-term development, helping people to help themselves;

- responds to emergencies, by offering immediate help;

- identifies poverty's causes and raises public awareness of them, encouraging people to 'challenge the structures, policies and attitudes that reinforce inequality';

- speaks out for poor communities, explaining poverty's underlying causes and challenging governments and international bodies to adopt policies that promote equality and justice.

 GOING DEEPER

What do we mean by developed and developing countries?

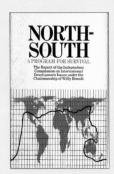

The difference between developed and developing countries is sometimes called the north–south divide. The Brandt Report (1980), the most complete study of world poverty to date, uses this shorthand in its title: *North–South: A Program for Survival.*

The word 'north' here is used to describe those countries with advanced economies dependent on services and manufacture for their prosperity, i.e. the developed nations of western Europe, North America and Australasia. (Although Australasia is in the southern hemisphere, it is classed as belonging to the wealthy north.) The rich northern hemisphere contains only 25 per cent of the world's population but consumes 80 per cent of the world's resources. The remaining 75 per cent of the world has access to only 20 per cent of its resources. Many Christians believe that this disproportionate consumption of the world's resources put those of us who belong to the rich north in the position of the rich people whose behaviour Jesus condemned.

Most people in the poor countries of the '**Global South**' work in agriculture: around 75 per cent of them work on the land as opposed to 4 per cent in the UK. Despite this focus on producing food, the developing world is characterized by a high level of malnutrition (although the world produces enough food to give every person on the planet enough to eat: 3,000 calories a day). The people also lack clean drinking water and adequate medical care:

- a third of the world's population has no access to clean water;

- 2.4 billion have no access to adequate sanitation;

- without proper medical care, many babies die in early childhood and life expectancy is low (about 50 years compared to 70 or more years in developed countries).

People in the developing world also suffer from a high level of illiteracy. The one billion or so who are illiterate find it difficult to better themselves and escape poverty.

Malnutrition and natural disasters

About 20 million people a year die from malnutrition. These deaths don't occur because there are too many mouths to feed but because the best land and the food that it produces are not where they are needed most. Population density is much greater in western Europe (96 people per square kilometre than in Africa (18 people per square kilometre) but the land is also far more fertile. Tragically, in the rich northern countries, there is over-production of food, which later often has to be destroyed. The USA (with 6 per cent of the world's population) consumes (or disposes of) 30 per cent of the world's food.

Those in the poorest parts of the world are also particularly susceptible to natural disasters and are less able to deal with them.

Campaign for trade justice

International trade is regulated by rules and treaties, which campaigners for organizations such as Make Poverty History claim favour the wealthy nations and international companies at the expense of poor countries and their people. They want to see this injustice corrected; they want **trade justice**.

The vicious circle of poverty: the campaign's version

Many people struggle to increase their earnings, however hard they work (over 50 per cent of the world's people live on less than $2 each a day). This enforced poverty is caused by the rich countries' domination of world trade through the World Trade Organization (WTO), the World Bank and the International Monetary Fund (IMF). These organizations force poor countries to open up their markets to competition from foreign imports and businesses. They also prevent poor countries from protecting their vulnerable farmers and industries (even though such 'protectionism' is common in the rich countries). This lack of protection means

that farms and businesses often fail and basic public services are bought out by investors seeking a quick profit. People find themselves employed as cheap labour with poor, under-regulated working conditions.

The origins of the debts of poor countries

In the 1970s and 1980s, many poor countries borrowed money to fund development projects (such as power plants and water distribution systems). They hoped that high prices for their commodities (crude oil, natural gas, gold, silver, aluminium, copper, coffee, cocoa, wheat, soybeans, etc.) would enable them to pay these loans back. However, commodity prices fell and interest rates rose, leaving many countries unable to repay their debts. This situation led to protests in rich nations as well as poor countries. At the 1998 G8 summit (the G8 is the group of eight of the world's richest nations), protestors criticized a situation where more was being taken in interest than was being given in aid (£3 taken for every £1 given). The effects have been devastating: for example, in Malawi more is spent on servicing debt than on health, despite the fact that 20 per cent of the population is HIV positive. In Zambia, debt repayments exceed what is spent on education.

Trade justice and free trade: not as simple as it seems

The campaign demands 'trade justice' not '**free trade**' on the assumption that industries in poor countries need protection as they are growing. Otherwise greedy foreign multinational companies will destroy them by competing unfairly.

However, Stephen Pollard, in *The Times*, 23 May 2005, puts a counter-argument that tariff protection perpetuates the inefficient use of resources. Evidence to support this view is provided by Malaysia, Singapore, Thailand, South Korea and India. As long as they retained tariffs, they remained poor. Their prosperity has increased since they abandoned them. In the 1980s, these countries' incomes per head were in the range of $700 to $7,000; in 2005, they were in the range of $2000 to $21,000. This increase in prosperity came about because the parts of their economies that were uncompetitive dwindled and those that successfully expanded attracted overseas investment.

The two campaigns Drop the Debt (www.jubileedebtcampaign.org.uk) and More and Better (www.moreandbetter.org/en/), among others, argue that if the debt burden is reduced, aid is effectively increased. However, many commentators are wary of simply reducing debt or increasing aid because the benefit might go to the (often corrupt) minority of people that run indebted nations. It might also encourage those leaders to continue to govern poorly. For example, one reason most of the people of Nigeria, one of the world's oil-rich nations, remain poor might be because Nigerian governments have been corrupt.

The economist Hernando de Soto argues in his influential book *The Mystery of Capital* that making a country prosperous is relatively easy: it 'needs only security of life and property, and markets in which property rights can be valued and traded. The West's prosperity is built on property and the rule of law; it is the denial of those rights which causes poverty and prevents growth.'

In many poor countries, it is very difficult to do business. For example, in Canada and Australia you can legally set up (incorporate) a company in 2 days, but this process takes 16 days in Algeria, 153 days in Mozambique or 203 in Haiti. Also, the cost of setting up a company in Denmark is nothing, whereas it costs 1,268 per cent of the average income in Sierra Leone or the deposit of the

equivalent of 18 years' average income in Ethiopia. In Nigeria, recording a property sale involves 21 procedures and takes 274 days.

The Grameen Bank

The economist Muhammad Yunus found that many very poor people in Bangladesh trying to start a business had little chance of success because of the very high rates of interest money-lenders charged. So, Yunus decided to provide 'micro-loans' – small loans at very low rates of interest. He started the Grameen Bank Project in 1976 to make the loans available.

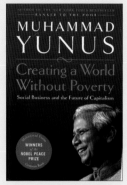

Today, the bank is lending in almost 70,000 villages and has more than 6 million customers. Most of its borrowers are women and over 98 per cent of its loans are repaid (far more than a British high-street bank). For this work, Yunus

'**[Marjina Begum] had seen** how some of the women in her village had benefited from their relationship with Grameen and finally, with her living conditions at rock bottom, Marjina decided to risk it and take out a loan of 2,500 taka (about £20). She used the money to start her own sewing business and began to produce and sell bags.

A year later, having repaid her initial borrowing, she took out a larger loan, which she used to buy a goat, some hens and other livestock.

Subsequently she took out a housing loan and built a home for herself and her family. A series of small microfinance loans, combined with determination and hard work, have lifted the Begum family out of poverty: "It feels good to earn money; I am no longer dependent on my husband. I now have self-confidence," Marjina told me.'

(Andrew Mitchell, Shadow Secretary for State, International Development (2006))

was awarded the 2006 Nobel Peace Prize.

Yunus' approach is in marked contrast to the grand-scale projects (such as Make Poverty History) that may have difficulty in succeeding, not least because they often have to deal with corrupt governments. The Grameen Bank takes the solution of poverty to its grassroots. In doing so, Yunus shows that the poor are not just pitiable cases hoping for charity from rich nations but are, rather, thwarted business people needing only a small amount of help to transform their lives.

What the Churches teach

Roman Catholic Church

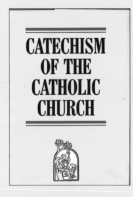

A summary of Roman Catholic teaching about poverty can be found in the *Catechism of the Catholic Church* (1993). It states that 'God blesses those who come to the aid of the poor and rebukes those who turn away from them'. It also teaches that 'the Church's love for the poor is a part of her constant tradition' and 'Love for the poor is incompatible with immoderate love of riches or their selfish use'. Moreover, quoting St John Chrysostom, it adds that 'not to enable the poor to share in our goods is to steal from them and deprive them of life. The goods we possess are not ours, but theirs.'

Church of England

The Church of England, like the Roman Catholic Church, is concerned with economic justice, and resolutions of the **General Synod** reflect this concern. Take,

for example, a resolution from 1981: 'The Synod [believes] that, as a matter of common humanity and of our mutual interest in survival, the world requires a new and more equitable system of economic relationships between nations.'

The Church of England also teaches that its members should see themselves as 'stewards' of creation (an idea based on Genesis 1.26), which means that they must use its resources responsibly. See the Church of England website (www.cofe.anglican.org/info/funding/stewardship.htm)

The Church of England also connects this stewardship with the belief that the best way to show how much we appreciate God's love for us is to 'love back': 'We love because he first loved us' (1 John 4.19). And we love God back by practising 'Christian stewardship', which 'may . . . be defined as the response which we the Church, collectively and individually, are called to make to God for all that he has given us and done for us, above all in Jesus Christ' (www.cofe.anglican.org/info/funding/stewardship.html).

The General Synod of the Church of England makes statements on ethical issues

SUMMARY

1 The different kinds of aid are emergency aid, long-term aid and prophetic aid.

2 Jesus taught extensively about wealth and its proper use.

3 Jesus had little personal property himself and commended 'travelling light' to his disciples. The earliest Christian communities seem to have practised common ownership of property. Monastic communities continue living in this way.

4 The major Christian Churches are notable for their concern with the relief of poverty and suffering in our own society and internationally.

5 The Western Churches operate in societies that are materialistic.

6 Judaism saw human beings as stewards of the earth's resources.

7 Jesus praised those who gave freely to the less fortunate and condemned those who ignored the suffering of the poor.

8 Jesus did not always insist on using resources to help the poor, though. He commended extravagance in some circumstances. Therefore, Christians need to establish priorities.

9 Jesus may well have criticized the wealthy because very few people were wealthy in his society, and those who were rich often exploited the poor. The north–south divide today provides a modern example of similar extremes of wealth and poverty.

10 Individual Christians in the UK usually contribute to the alleviation of poverty through national charities, principally Christian Aid, Tearfund and CAFOD.

11 Christian Aid helps all people, not only Christians. Although involved in emergency disaster relief, its principal work is in helping people to improve their lives and deal with the causes of poverty and injustice. It works with 'partners', local community groups and church organizations.

12 Tearfund works through local partners. Its principal areas of involvement are community development, disaster response, speaking out and helping families to be self-reliant.

13 CAFOD is the Catholic Agency for Overseas Development. Between 85 and 90 per cent of CAFOD's funds go to programmes to reduce global poverty and injustice.

GOING DEEPER

14 The difference between rich countries and poor ones is often called the north–south divide because the richest countries are predominantly in the northern hemisphere.

15 The rich 25 per cent of the world's population living in the northern hemisphere consumes 80 per cent of the earth's resources. Many Christians believe that this fact places those of us who live in the rich north in the same position as the exploitative rich that Jesus condemned.

16 The poorer, developing nations are characterized by malnutrition, a lack of clean drinking water and medical care, illiteracy and low per capita income.

17 Campaigners for better conditions for the poorer countries contend that poorer nations are kept poor by exploitative trade.

18 Campaigners argue that trade justice is the best way to help them.

19 Writing off the debts of poor countries may effectively increase the aid that they receive but this action might benefit only a corrupt ruling class.

20 Some argue that trade justice is not the answer. Protecting the industries of poorer countries from competition with those of richer nations might encourage the inefficient use of resources to continue.

21 Economists such as de Soto argue that the rule of law and right to property are the best ways to secure prosperity.

22 The provision of micro-loans at reasonable interest rates appears to be an effective way of helping people in poorer countries to set up small businesses and create employment and economic growth.

23 The *Catechism of the Catholic Church* summarizes a substantial body of Roman Catholic teaching about poverty.

24 The Church of England's concern for justice for the poor is reflected in resolutions of the General Synod.

REVISION QUESTIONS

1 How would you describe Jesus' basic attitude to wealth?

2 What kind of ownership of property was practised by the earliest Christian communities?

3 What is the basic attitude of the main Christian Churches today towards wealth?

4 What is meant by 'materialistic' when it is used to describe modern, advanced Western societies?

5 How did Judaism see the relationship of human beings to the earth's resources?

6 How did Jesus regard those (a) who helped the poor and (b) those who ignored the needs of the poor?

7 How did Jesus regard the actions of the woman who anointed him with expensive oil before his death? What might this teach modern Christians?

8 What might have influenced Jesus' attitude to the wealthy in his society?

9 Who, in general terms, are the 'wealthy' in the modern world? Give reasons for your opinion.

10 What is the basis for believing that the amount of today's wealth is often gained at the expense of the poor?

11 What are the different kinds of aid?

GOING DEEPER

12 What is meant by the north–south divide?

13 Give examples of some of the problems experienced by poorer nations.

14 Why might freeing poor nations of their debt make a difference?

15 What are micro-loans and how can they help people in poorer countries?

16 How much of the work of the principal Christian charities in the UK involves responding to emergencies?

17 Outline the ways in which Christian Aid and Tearfund work overseas.

18 What is meant by 'speaking out' or 'prophetic' work?

Personal stories

A pensioner fell victim to two bogus water board officials. The pair had been seen hanging around a block of flats by the elderly woman, so she opened her back door to speak with them over the railings.

Police said the men told the woman there was a water problem in the area and one of them came into her flat. He spent 20 minutes pretending to look for a stopcock to turn her water off.

He ran away when the pensioner phoned a friend. She then discovered her bedroom had been searched and police believe the second man stole cash from one of her drawers.

Witnesses described two men seen around the block of flats at the time and another person reported seeing three men speed off in a four-door silver Mercedes.

Mark Nepokroeff practised medicine in Niagara County, New York, although he hadn't completed medical school. Despite the fact his diploma was fake, he was employed by the State of New York, which gave him a medical licence, and by the federal government. His main work was to assess workers' compensation for injury claims and claims for disability grants. His punishment: four months in federal prison and $233,439 in restitution.

Nepokroeff's attitude towards disabled people was astonishing. He stated: 'There is no such thing as a totally disabled person', 'Most people on workers' compensation just want a free vacation' and 'Most people on workers' compensation are fraudulent.' His response to hearing that one of his workers' compensation patients had jumped out of a top window of Erie County Medical Center was to laugh and say: 'Well, his problems are over.'

(www.injuredworker.org/insurance_fraud.htm)

Glossary

capital punishment the death penalty

conscience defined by St Thomas Aquinas (*c.* 1225–74) as 'the mind of man making moral judgements'; sometimes described as an 'inward voice'

crime an act against the law

deterrence something that puts people off committing crime, e.g. the risk of being caught

forgiveness the decision to stop resenting someone and not to take revenge for something he or she did to hurt you; forgiveness can lead to reconciliation

indictable describes a serious offence. Involves a jury trial, if a preliminary hearing determines there is a case to answer. It is in contrast to minor offences which are called 'summary offences' and are dealt with 'summarily', without a jury trial

justice the quality of being fair and unbiased, to do what is right

lex talionis inflicting a 'like' penalty for a crime, i.e. taking a 'life for a life'

penal concerned with punishment (related to the word 'penalty')

punishment a penalty given for any crime or offence

recidivism the tendency of many offenders to return to crime again and again

rehabilitation process whereby a criminal is restored to a normal life in society

reconciliation the restoration of agreement or a good relationship between people who had a disagreement or a bad relationship

retribution wronged individuals sometimes demand retribution (being 'paid back' or 'revenged') for the harm they have suffered; in its simplest form, they seek 'an eye for an eye'

Discussion

- If you were judging the case involving the bogus officials how would you deal with the two men? Look at this case again after you have read the rest of the topic.
- Why do you think that Nepokroeff was given a light prison sentence but a big fine?

INTRODUCTION AND MAIN POINTS

Before you read the rest of this topic, cast your mind back to your earliest memory of doing wrong.

Let me give you a personal example. I remember at the age of 10 putting an insulated screwdriver across a live light socket to see whether there would be sparks. There were sparks, and notches were burnt into the metal shaft of the screwdriver and I blew the light's fuse. This all happened before I went to school one morning. My wrongdoing was on my mind all day while I was at school. When my mother collected me, she asked me what had happened. Her main concern was that I hadn't hurt myself. She wasn't really annoyed with me at all. I think I learned, though, that what I had done was really stupid and dangerous. I certainly had no intention of doing anything like that again.

These early experiences of doing silly or wrong things are very important to our development. If we have wise parents, they teach us in our early years to look after our safety and to get on well with other people.

What they and other responsible adults – for instance, teachers – are doing is helping to develop and form our **conscience**, which enables us to distinguish right from wrong behaviour.

As we grow older, they teach us not just how to behave at home and school but how to behave in wider society. We learn not to take goods from shops without paying for them and not to use violence against other people, even when they irritate us.

However, some people don't learn these lessons very well or ignore them. In their teens, or even earlier, they start to offend not only against the rules of 'good behaviour' but also against the law. Such people are 'young offenders'. They have crossed the barrier from behaving badly to committing **crime**. But this does not mean that they will be treated in the same way as adults who commit crime. In the UK, children under the age of 10 are not considered to be capable of being responsible for a crime, and young people under the age of 18 who commit crimes are treated separately from adults.

Criminal behaviour: penal issues

Criminal behaviour raises three main **penal** issues:

1 stopping crime;

2 the treatment of criminals;

3 balancing the interests of the victims of crime with those who have committed crimes.

Stopping crime

Deterrence, stopping crime, is most people's principal concern. It is often argued that this is best achieved by:

- deploying more police (making it more likely that criminals will be caught);

- making imprisonment the penalty for more crimes and making prison sentences longer (in the hope that criminals will be put off by the prospect of losing their freedom, or doing so for a substantial time).

The treatment of criminals

- Those whose principal concern is with the victims of crime favour **retribution**.

- Those whose main interest is the criminals themselves favour reformation and **rehabilitation**.

However, a wide spectrum of opinion exists. The supporters of retribution may also care about the treatment of criminals and the supporters of rehabilitation may also be bothered about the victims of crime. It is a question of balance.

Retribution

A desire for retribution is provoked in many people by the actions of serial killers or those who kill children, or by any crimes of violence towards the weak and vulnerable. Financial frauds, whereby ordinary people have their savings stolen, also have the same effect. People want those who died or those who were deprived to be revenged and they demand that the public receive protection from such criminals. They believe that the criminals should 'pay' for their crimes.

Reformation and rehabilitation

An awareness of prison conditions and the disadvantaged social background of many prisoners makes some people focus on social reform. They believe that improved 'life chances' through better education, better job opportunities and support for troubled families might 'breed' less crime.

Those who favour rehabilitation believe that those who have committed crimes should be helped to 'mend their ways' and reform their behaviour. Once this process has been successfully completed they should be helped to find their place in society again, i.e. receive rehabilitation.

Balancing the interests of the victims and the criminals

This balance is notoriously difficult to strike. On the one hand, too much emphasis on retribution might simply make the offender feel more remote from ordinary human society and, if the offender is imprisoned, even more likely to reoffend when he or she is let out. Therefore, one school of thought sees the main purpose of the Prison Service as that of preparing offenders for an ordinary life in society (rehabilitation) and to prevent **recidivism**.

On the other hand, if too much stress is laid on the rehabilitation of the offender, it appears that society is more concerned with criminals than with the victims of crime. If this happens, the public feels at greater risk and criminals might not be sufficiently deterred.

Ultimately, people's attitudes are most likely to be affected by how closely they have been touched by criminal behaviour. Crime victims might be more likely to want retribution.

Extreme punishments

Capital punishment

Since 1965, the penalty of **capital punishment** has not been available to British courts, and British parliaments have consistently rejected its reintroduction. However, opinion polls show wide public support for it, especially

when a particularly violent murder has received blanket media coverage.

Basic arguments in favour of capital punishment

- It demonstrates society's revulsion at the taking of life.
- It deters people from committing murder.
- It protects the general population because the murderer will never re-enter society to reoffend.
- It is appropriate that those who have taken life should forfeit their lives on the principle of 'a life for a life' (***lex talionis***).
- Revenge is a natural human response, especially to something as serious as murder.
- The death of the murderer helps the family of the victim to 'get over' the crime or 'experience closure' (a term that has become popular).

Basic arguments against capital punishment

- Although it is 'state sanctioned', it remains the 'taking of life', i.e. murder in itself.
- All life is sacred (see the note on 'sanctity of life' on pages 32 and 37).
- Innocent people might be executed and such mistakes cannot be undone.
- Statistics do not indicate that the death penalty has any deterrent effect.
- In the case of murders carried out by terrorists, executing them might turn them into martyrs, which could make a political situation worse.
- The time that elapses between conviction and execution (because of appeals), which can run into years, amounts to 'cruel and unnatural punishment' – the whole process of the death penalty is, therefore, inhumane.
- There is the question of who can be expected to carry out the court's sentence of execution.
- Murder is often the result of domestic psychological pressures that have become unbearable – in 77 per cent of cases the victim knew the murderer.

Mutilation

Some Muslim societies governed, for example, by sharia law have **punishments** that reflect a strict *lex talionis* approach, e.g. a thief might have a hand or foot amputated. Western societies tend to react to news of such punishments as 'barbaric'. In fact, such punishments existed in Western societies before attitudes and fashions changed.

THE CHRISTIAN VIEW

Jesus was not directly concerned with social issues like crime and punishment. However, Christians have tended to take Jesus' teaching about how we should

relate to each other and apply it to social issues.

Different biblical passages can be used in support of both retribution and rehabilitation, and some individual passages support both approaches.

Using the Bible in support of retribution

There is a Christian tradition of retribution, which reflects the *lex talionis* teaching of the Old Testament: 'Anyone who maims another shall suffer the same injury in return: fracture for fracture, eye for eye, tooth for tooth; the injury inflicted is the injury to be suffered' (Leviticus 24.19–20). But Jesus explicitly rejects the idea of revenge (see Matthew 5.38).

However, Jesus seems to favour retribution in some circumstances. For example, in the parable of the unforgiving servant (Matthew 18.23–35), a king (God) forgives one of his servants (a sinner) huge debts. The king changes his mind when the debtor (sinner) does not forgive his subordinates (other sinners) their much smaller debts. The moral of this story is that unforgiveness (and unfairness) is rewarded with retribution.

St Paul seems to tend towards retribution. At the beginning of Romans 13, he states that everyone should be subject to 'the governing authorities', which potential wrongdoers should fear. Then the authorities, as servants of God, will execute 'wrath on the wrongdoer' – a state of affairs that Paul does not criticize.

Using the Bible in support of reformation and rehabilitation

Jesus' teaching and example of forgiveness (see page 93), however, seem to support a legal system that favours reformation and rehabilitation.

His treatment of a woman caught committing adultery – an offence punishable by death at that time – also supports rehabilitation. He forgave her unconditionally but advised her: 'Go your way; and from now on do not sin again' (i.e. be reformed; John 8.11). Obeying this advice would lead to her being rehabilitated into society. However, it must be admitted that in this story Jesus is primarily concerned with personal behaviour and whether anyone has the right to judge someone else. He does not approve of the woman's conduct (she should sin no more), yet he puts her accusers on the spot by asking the man among them who was 'without sin' to be the first to begin her execution by casting the 'first' stone. The accusers drift away, aware that none of them is sinless.

Copyright © Richard Smith

Forgiveness

Forgiveness is one of Jesus' principal teachings. When Peter asks Jesus how often he should forgive others, Jesus replies, 'Not seven times, but, I tell you, seventy-seven times' (Matthew 18.22). Jesus also offers the supreme example of forgiveness when – as he is dying on the cross – he says, 'Father, forgive them; for they do not know what they are doing' (Luke 23.34).

This teaching can seem very demanding. It is natural for human beings to hit out at those who hurt them, and to want retribution. We might find that we can follow Jesus' teaching if the hurt is small, for instance when someone teases us or spills juice on our new clothes. But how do we forgive rapists or people who murder children? We want those who have committed such crimes to 'pay for them' – to make reparation – yet the crimes seem too big for reparation to be possible.

Christians believe that forgiveness is only possible with God's help in cases of child murder, serial killing or genocide. God operates at a different level: Jesus freely forgives those who cannot earn forgiveness (e.g. those who crucified him). Christians also believe that the power of Jesus' forgiveness (something freely given, 'grace') is present with them when they forgive someone who has committed a great wrong. A woman named Marie was killed in the 1987 Enniskillen bombing in Northern Ireland. Grace enabled her father, Gordon Wilson, to say that he would pray every night for the men responsible for the bombing. There are also examples of those who survived Second World War concentration camps being reconciled with their guards. One example, the story of a Dutch woman called Corrie ten Boom, can be found at www.humiliationstudies.org/documents/DanaherCorrieTenBoomsStory.pdf.

✳ GOING DEEPER

How crime is punished: current approaches

Punishments vary in their emphasis. In general terms, imprisonment is retributive and suspended sentences and community service are more concerned with reformation and rehabilitation.

Factors that affect the kind of sentence imposed are:

- whether the offence is **indictable**;
- whether it is a first offence;
- whether it involved violence or not;
- the age of the offender.

Experimental approaches: restorative justice

The concept of restorative **justice** has attracted the attention of governments and reformers of the criminal justice system. Everyone recognizes that far too many offenders reoffend after they have been in prison or done community service. Restorative justice aims to bring offenders and victims of crime together, so that offenders can recognize what they have done (which might make them less willing to reoffend) and have the opportunity to make amends. Meetings of this type might also lead to **reconciliation**.

Zacchaeus promised to return money to the people he had cheated

Copyright © Richard Smith

This approach is modelled on many biblical stories, e.g. the story of Zacchaeus, the tax collector, who made his money from creaming off some of the taxes that he collected (see Luke 19.1–10). When Jesus asked to eat with him, Zacchaeus was suddenly filled with remorse at his behaviour. He promised to give back four times as much as he had stolen and to give half his possessions to the poor. After thinking about his crimes, Zacchaeus wanted to *restore* (hence *restorative* justice) relationships with those he had cheated, and to do so by giving back more than he had taken.

Review this list of penalties and assess where they fall in the spectrum between retribution and rehabilitation.

- *Imprisonment*: those over 21 can be sent to prison.
- *Young offender institutions*: those under 21 can be sent to one of these.
- *Suspended sentence*: a custodial (prison) sentence which is 'suspended' from operation unless the offender commits another imprisonable offence during the period of the suspended sentence. This type of sentence might be given when someone has not committed an offence before or when there are mitigating circumstances (e.g. if the offender has children to support).
- *Fine*: commonly given for non-indictable offences, e.g. parking and speeding offences. They are usually geared to the severity of the offence and, often, to the ability of the offender to pay.
- *Community service*: offenders over the age of 17 can be made to do unpaid work for between 40 and 240 hours instead of going to prison.
- *Conditional discharge*: the offender is made to promise not to reoffend, and is required to keep the promise.
- *Attendance centres*: usually offenders aged between 10 and 16 (and sometimes between 17 and 20) are made to attend centres for three hours on a Saturday morning. These centres are often staffed by off-duty police and they organize activities that include sport, citizenship skills, first aid, DIY, home electronics, driver education, personal health and victim awareness.
- *Probation*: only those above the age of 17 can be put on probation. The offender is free but under the supervision of a probation officer.
- *Care*: some criminals under 18 (juveniles) can be put under the care of the local authority.
- *Caution*: sometimes, when a relatively minor offence is involved, provided an offender admits his or her guilt, the offender is allowed to escape prosecution and is simply 'cautioned'.

Here are some examples of restorative justice.

- *Victim–offender mediation programmes*: both parties consent to a meeting designed to help offenders to make voluntary reparations to victims. The offender usually admits to causing harm, gives an apology and some sort of explanation of events.

- *Family-group conferencing*: a form of mediation that brings together the victim and the offender with their families and supporters, as well as wider community representatives. It focuses on the wider picture and breakdowns in the offender's social situation, especially in the case of young people, and is viewed as a powerful tool for achieving reconciliation and social integration. This approach was first used in New Zealand with young people.

Organizations campaigning for the rights of prisoners

The Howard League for Penal Reform

The Howard Association was formed in honour of the prison reformer John Howard in 1866, almost 80 years after his death. It was dedicated to the reform of prisons and the abolition of capital punishment. It merged in 1921 with the Penal Reform League to form the Howard League for Penal Reform. Today, it continues to work to prevent deaths in custody and suicides in prison.

Student supporters of the Howard League demonstrate for prison reform at the University of Westminster

Candles and barbed wire, the symbols of Amnesty International

Amnesty International

Amnesty International is a worldwide movement dedicated to campaigning to promote the human rights that are laid out in the Universal Declaration of Human Rights and similar international documents. It is independent of any government and impartial to any political persuasion or religious creed. It is financed largely by subscriptions and donations from its worldwide membership.

It aims to 'to free all prisoners of conscience; ensure fair and prompt trials for political prisoners; abolish the death penalty, torture and other cruel treatment of prisoners; end political killings and "disappearances"; and oppose human rights abuses by opposition groups' (see www.amnesty.org).

Amnesty International has a membership of about one million in 162 countries and territories. Its range of activities includes public demonstrations, letter-writing, human-rights education, fundraising concerts, individual appeals and global campaigns.

Christian Churches and crime

Capital punishment is the issue that most concerns the Christian Churches. They are also involved in welfare work in prisons through the system of prison chaplaincies and advocate a balance between restorative justice and rehabilitation.

Church of England

The Church of England is opposed to the reintroduction of the death penalty. In July 1983, the General Synod debated capital punishment and the following motion was carried: 'That this Synod would deplore the reintroduction of capital punishment into the UK's sentencing policy.' This subject has not been debated by Synod since 1983.

Whenever the criminal justice system (the system of courts, approaches to sentencing and treatment of offenders) is being considered by Parliament, the Church of England is asked to contribute to the debate. The Church does this through the contributions of the bishops who are members of the House of Lords and through submissions to committees of Parliament.

For example, in 1999 the General Synod commented on the government's proposal to develop restorative justice programmes. The Synod supported such programmes because they 'enshrine the biblical principles of holding offenders responsible for their crimes, addressing the needs of victims, and enhancing the protection of the public'. In particular, this included welcoming 'efforts to prevent 15- and 16-year-olds being remanded into prison custody by offering constructive alternatives in the community'.

Roman Catholic Church

The Roman Catholic Church is also opposed to capital punishment and seeks its universal abolition: 'The Holy See has consistently sought the abolition of the death penalty and his Holiness Pope John Paul II has personally and indiscriminately appealed on numerous occasions in order that such sentences should be commuted to a lesser punishment' (see *Declaration of the Holy See to the First World Congress on the Death Penalty*, 2001).

However, the Roman Catholic Church also recognizes the need to balance the protection of society with the rehabilitation of the offender (note the italic text in the quotation

from the teaching of the US Catholic bishops in 2000):

> We cannot and will not tolerate behavior that threatens lives and violates the rights of others. We believe in responsibility, accountability, and legitimate punishment. Those who harm others or damage property must be held accountable for the hurt they have caused. The community has a right to establish and enforce laws to protect people and to advance the common good.
>
> At the same time, a Catholic approach does not give up on those who violate these laws. We believe that both victims and offenders are children of God. Despite their very different claims on society, their lives and dignity should be protected and respected. *We seek justice, not vengeance. We believe punishment must have clear purposes: protecting society and rehabilitating those who violate the law.*
> (United States Conference of Catholic Bishops)

The Roman Catholic bishops also draw attention to – and deplore – the fact that, in the USA, a greater proportion of people from ethnic minorities than from the white population are likely to end up in prison, which is also the case in the UK.

Ethnic minorities are more likely to be imprisoned

There is statistical evidence that ethnic minorities are far more likely to be imprisoned.

In June 1999, the rate of imprisonment per 100,000 of the general population in England and Wales was:

- 1,265 for black people;
- 184 for white people;
- 147 for South Asians.

(For further information see the Howard League website: www.howardleague.org.)

There is a similar pattern in the USA. In 2000, of those in prison:

- 49 per cent were African Americans (although they account for only 12 per cent of the US population; in fact, 10 per cent of male African Americans are in prison, on probation or on parole);
- 19 per cent were Hispanic Americans (although they make up just 9 per cent of the US population).

(www.usccb.org/sdwp/criminal.shtml#introduction)

SUMMARY

1 'Doing wrong' and 'committing a crime' are not necessarily the same thing.

2 Young people under 18 are treated separately from adults; children under the age of 10 cannot be held responsible for crimes.

3 Crime prevention, the treatment of criminals and balancing the interests of the victims and the criminals are the principal issues, but not in equal measure.

4 Deterrence and the protection of the public concern people most. They want police to enforce the law and catch criminals because they hope that efficient policing, combined with appropriate penalties, will deter people from committing crimes.

5 However, there is also support for a variety of types of reform:

  (a) Supporters of social reform claim that the best long-term solution to crime is the improvement of people's 'life chances', through better education, the provision of job opportunities and support for families in trouble.

  (b) Those who want to see the reform of offenders argue that prison must be a place where criminals are rehabilitated (i.e. enabled to take their place constructively in society), so they won't commit any more crimes. This approach might mean that the prisons themselves have to be reformed.

6 The purpose of punishment, especially the use of imprisonment, is the issue over which there is most disagreement. Some are concerned that criminals should be locked away to protect the public and that offenders should 'pay' for their crimes (retribution), while others want to see positive change in criminals' behaviour (reform and rehabilitation). Everyone is concerned to prevent criminals from reoffending (recidivism).

7 However, the question is not one of *either* retribution *or* reform and rehabilitation. Most of the public are concerned to see punishment for crime *and* the reform and rehabilitation of the offender. People vary over whether they are *more* concerned with retribution than rehabilitation and vice versa. Those who have been touched by criminal behaviour are more likely to favour retribution.

8 Christian teaching can be found in support of both opinions. Some point to Old Testament passages that seem to favour retribution (e.g. Leviticus 24.19). However, Jesus seems to have contradicted this approach (Matthew 5.38). He also stressed the need for repeated forgiveness (Matthew 18.21–22).

GOING DEEPER

9 Punishments vary in their emphasis. Imprisonment has a mainly retributive purpose (although it is also be for the public's protection). Suspended sentences, fines and community service orders are intended to foster rehabilitation and reformation.

10 Restorative justice brings offenders and crime victims together, so that offenders recognize what they have done and have the opportunity to make amends.

11 This approach is modelled on the story of the biblical Zacchaeus, a tax collector who wanted to restore what he had stolen to his victims.

12 Examples of restorative justice include victim–offender mediation programmes and family-group conferencing.

13 The Howard League for Penal Reform, founded in 1866, was dedicated to prison reform and abolishing capital punishment; it continues to work to prevent deaths in custody and suicides in prison.

14 Amnesty International is a worldwide organization which campaigns for human rights. Among its goals, it aims to free prisoners of conscience and abolish the death penalty.

15 The Church of England opposes the reintroduction of the death penalty and contributes to parliamentary debates about the criminal justice system. The General Synod has given support to restorative justice programmes.

16 The Roman Catholic Church seeks the universal abolition of capital punishment.

17 The Roman Catholic Church also recognizes the need to balance the protection of society with the rehabilitation of the offender.

18 There is statistical evidence – in England and Wales and in the USA – that ethnic minorities are more likely to be imprisoned.

REVISION QUESTIONS

1 What is meant by the term crime?

2 Explain the terms reform, rehabilitation, retribution, *lex talionis* and recidivism.

3 When did capital punishment cease to be a penalty in the UK?

4 Quote two biblical texts used in favour of retribution and explain how they are used.

5 Quote two biblical texts used in favour of rehabilitation and explain how they are used.

6 What, according to penal reformers, may increase the incidence of crime?

GOING DEEPER

7 Name two penalties that reflect a rehabilitation approach to crime and punishment. Give reasons for your choices.

8 Which penalty most reflects a retributive approach to crime and punishment? Give reasons for your choice.

9 What is the Howard League for Penal Reform?

10 What does the Roman Catholic Church teach about capital punishment?

Personal stories

The Berks, Bucks & Oxon Wildlife Trust (BBOWT) had hoped that the expert panel would listen to their arguments about the need to include measures to safeguard wildlife. However, although the expert panel did acknowledge the need to protect and enhance the region's **biodiversity**, they actually proposed even more houses than were already planned (an additional 62,000 in the South East as a whole on top of the original 580,000).

'This is potentially disastrous for our wildlife,' said Philippa Lyons, Chief Executive of BBOWT. 'We recognize that growth needs to happen and that there will be significant development in the South East. However, the scale of development originally set out in the draft plan was already pushing the limit of the region's environmental capacity.'

(www.wildaboutbritain.co.uk/forums/environment-forum)

John inherited a small organic farm from his father, who used to keep a large herd of cows for milk production. The herd had to be slaughtered during a foot-and-mouth epidemic, which caused his father to despair and commit suicide. A large agricultural company has made John a substantial offer for his farm, with the intention of establishing a chicken 'factory farm'. John has a wife and family of three young children to support but is passionately opposed to anything other than organic farming methods.

Glossary

acid rain gases produced by power stations, factories and cars (especially nitrogen oxides and sulphur dioxide) react with droplets of water in clouds to form acids, which fall as acid rain

agricultural run-off water containing fertilizers and pesticides draining from farmland into rivers, lakes and ponds

biodiversity the natural variety/diversity of species. Environmentalists want to preserve biodiversity

conservationists those wanting to conserve (protect) the environment from further pollution and damage

deforestation the destruction of forests

dominion means having power (literally 'lordship' from the Latin *dominus*, meaning 'lord')

environment the surroundings in which people live. If you live in the country, you live in a rural environment. If you live in a town, you live in an urban environment

environmentalists similar to conservationists but perhaps with more emphasis on speaking up for the environment against the risk of human exploitation

green the colour of living forests, etc. and used to describe anything environmental. It often prefixes other words, e.g. Greenpeace

Industrial Revolution the transformation of an economy from dependence on agriculture to dependence on industry; it began in Britain in the eighteenth century with the introduction of steam power in manufacture, followed by steam-powered transport

pollution occurs when the natural environment is contaminated by waste (e.g. chemicals or nuclear waste – by-products of nuclear power production)

stewards someone who looks after property for someone else. Stewardship as a Christian concept refers to human beings looking after the world for future generations

Discussion

- Why do you think that the environment has changed so much in the past 200 years and what are the principal features of this change?

- What are the main threats to the environment today?

- Are the interest of developers and conservationists bound to conflict?

⚜ INTRODUCTION AND MAIN POINTS

Copyright © Shutterstock

Copyright © Shutterstock

Imagine what your neighbourhood looked like a hundred years ago. You might have seen photographs or even paintings that can help you to visualize the scene. Almost certainly, there would have been fewer houses, more trees and no cars.

In a process that began with the **Industrial Revolution** over 200 years ago, the landscape of most Western countries has become dominated by the urban **environment** at the expense of the rural environment. Cities and towns have sprawled into the countryside and fields and woodland have been sacrificed to 'development'. Some parts of the landscape have been completely spoiled by industrial development and subsequent neglect. Farms have few people working on them and most aspects of agriculture are mechanized. Many animals are reared intensively and never see the light of day.

Copyright © Shutterstock

Scientists have also detected changes in our environment – especially in the atmosphere and, consequently, in the climate – that have the potential to affect the quality of life of every person and creature on the planet. The pessimists among them predict flooding in many parts of the world and the creation of deserts in others. The optimists rely on the hope that technological developments and changes in our behaviour can avert disaster.

Protecting the environment

An awareness of the need to protect the environment goes back over a century. In the UK, the National Trust has been an important conserver of the landscape, as well as historic buildings, since 1895. In the USA, there were calls for National Parks in the latter part of the nineteenth century and a law established these in 1917. Among a huge spectrum of environmental charities established since then, activist groups like Friends of the Earth and Greenpeace stand out (see page 108).

Environmental protectionists can claim substantial success. Rivers like the Thames are cleaner than they have been since Tudor times and now support many breeds of fish that had been absent for decades. However, developers and **conservationists** and **environmentalists** can be seen as being in perpetual rivalry, and the threats to the environment remain substantial and diverse.

Threats to the environment

The environment is threatened globally and locally. The greenhouse effect, **deforestation** and ozone depletion affect people all over the world. Other problems like excessive population growth, increases in the amount of traffic, building on 'green-field' sites, water pollution and the disposal of industrial waste tend to be more local in their effect, although they might eventually have an overall effect on the planet. **Pollution** – whether of land, rivers or seas – tends to have an effect well beyond the countries where it begins.

The greenhouse effect

The Earth relies upon the greenhouse effect for its survival. Gases in the atmosphere act as a kind of blanket – or greenhouse – preventing the heat that comes from the sun from radiating back into space. However, climate scientists have evidence that the emission of gases from human activity – burning fossils fuels, deforestation, etc. – is making the blanket too thick, permitting less heat to radiate out into space, which means that average temperatures are increasing, resulting in climate change

An illustration of the greenhouse effect
Taken from Nick Spencer and Robert White, *Christianity, Climate Change and Sustainable Living* (London: SPCK, 2007).

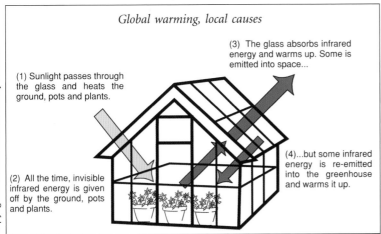

Global warming, local causes

(1) Sunlight passes through the glass and heats the ground, pots and plants.

(2) All the time, invisible infrared energy is given off by the ground, pots and plants.

(3) The glass absorbs infrared energy and warms up. Some is emitted into space...

(4)...but some infrared energy is re-emitted into the greenhouse and warms it up.

(seen in glaciers and polar ice melting, and water levels rising).

Ozone-layer depletion

Not only does the atmosphere keep heat in, so that the earth can sustain life, but it also insulates us from dangerous radiation produced by the sun. The part of the atmosphere that shields us is called the ozone layer. Its principal benefit is that it protects human beings from ultraviolet rays, which can cause skin cancer and cataracts. Unfortunately, gases in old-fashioned aerosol sprays and refrigerator fluid (chlorofluorocarbons (CFCs)) have seriously damaged it. Although their use is now banned, their effects could last for another century.

Ozone depletion is a good example of both the bad effect that industrialization has had on the environment and also of our ability to do something about it, although the benefits of a changed approach will take a long time to occur (you can search the US Environmental Protection Agency website for more information: www.epa.gov).

Deforestation

The period following the Second World War has seen a dramatic reduction in the extent of the Amazon rainforest and other equatorial forests (40 million acres a year, approximately an area the size of Great Britain, disappears each week). However, the extent of forest worldwide has actually increased (see 'The optimists' view' on page 107), although this increase has been of broadleaf woodlands and not rainforest.

The principal effect of rainforest destruction has been an increase in global warming. A report published by the Oxford-based Global Canopy project (www.globalcanopy. org/themedia/file/PDFs/Forests%20First% 20June%202007.pdf) showed that deforestation and burning of trees account for up to 25 per cent of global emissions of heat-trapping gases (transport and industry account for 14 per cent and aviation for 3 per cent).

The rainforests also contain about half the species that occur on Earth and their destruction can also lead to a loss of biodiversity. The preservation of biodiversity is regarded as worthwhile because valuable, naturally occurring drugs and chemicals are ultimately derived from the species that are threatened.

Depletion of forests can also cause flooding. For example, the mud-slides that killed thousands of Venezuelans in 1999 were partly caused by the loss of forests, which had formerly held soil together and prevented water flowing too rapidly off the land.

Pollution

Pollution takes many forms. It most commonly occurs when waste from industry, agriculture or our houses is disposed of carelessly. For example:

- burning fossil fuels to run cars or power stations produces carbon dioxide and carbon monoxide emissions, which may cause air quality to deteriorate and contribute to the greenhouse effect;
- sulphur dioxide emissions from coal-burning power stations pollute the atmosphere, causing **acid rain** to fall, which can kill trees, and fish in affected lakes and rivers. However, although such pollution is serious, effective measures to curb such emissions can be and are being taken. These types of pollution also tend to have a measurable effect within a short time-span:
- rivers might be polluted by **agricultural run-off**;
- household waste is usually disposed of in landfills (which may take a long time to rot away) or by incineration (which may increase emissions of carbon dioxide or sulphur dioxide).

Nuclear waste

Waste from nuclear power stations and the dismantling of nuclear weapons, in some ways, cause more concern. The waste can take centuries to become harmless, which poses the problem of where to dispose of it safely. People who live in the remote areas

Solar panels convert renewable energy from the sun into electricity. They are a clean and environmentally friendly alternative to polluting fossil fuels

that are usually chosen are wary of the risk of accidents or an increased likelihood of cancers developing in the local populace. Nuclear accidents like that at Chernobyl in 1986, which affected sites over a thousand miles away and continues to cause life-threatening health problems years later, strengthen the case for caution.

Human population growth

Human population growth, which is rapid in the developing world, has polluting effects. It often results in water shortages and over-cultivation of land, which later leads to the creation of new desert areas.

Plant and animal species might become endangered, since they have to compete with

How acid rain is formed

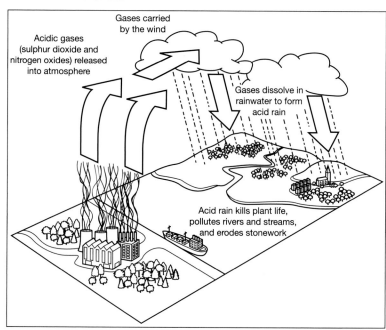

Gases carried by the wind

Acidic gases (sulphur dioxide and nitrogen oxides) released into atmosphere

Gases dissolve in rainwater to form acid rain

Acid rain kills plant life, pollutes rivers and streams, and erodes stonework

the expanding human population for increasingly scarce living space and food (discover more about species loss on the Internet, e.g. www. worldwildlife.org, www.bbc.co.uk).

THE CHRISTIAN VIEW

According to the Bible, God created the universe and gave human beings a special place in his creation. There are two accounts of creation: the first is given in Genesis 1; the second in Genesis 2. In the first creation story, the role of human beings is described in these terms: 'God blessed them [humankind], and God said to them, "Be fruitful and multiply, and fill the earth and *subdue it*; and *have dominion* over the fish of the sea and over the birds of the air and over every living thing that moves upon the earth"' (Genesis 1.28, emphasis added).

The second creation story begins with the creation of man and everything else is created to produce an 'environment' around him, which again implies the subordination of the creation to human beings. The fact that Adam is given the power to name everything reinforces this interpretation: 'and whatever the man called each living creature, that was its name' (Genesis 2.19).

'Dominion': a dangerous myth

The words 'subdue' and 'dominion' could imply an overwhelming power, and many modern writers have seen such language as influencing Western attitudes to the environment in a destructive way. It seems, they argue, to justify the exploitation of the earth. Thus, the anthropologist Desmond Morris – author of many influential books and broadcaster about human behaviour and zoology – accused religious leaders of feeding us with 'the dangerous myth that mankind is somehow above nature'. He sees this as a contributory factor in causing the 'ecological disaster' that the earth suffers from.

Stewardship

However, Christian writers would normally stress that the power humans possess is given to them on trust from God and that they are accountable to him for their conduct. They are **stewards** of the earth, not its creators or owners (see Topic 7, 'Wealth and poverty', page 84).

There are other biblical passages that can be used to support this belief. Psalm 8 not only describes the power that human beings have but also how that power is balanced by the sense of wonder and smallness in the face of the vastness of creation: 'When I look at your heavens, the work of your fingers, the moon and the stars that you have established; what are human beings that you are mindful of them, mortals that you care for them?' (Psalm 8.3–4)

There are also passages in Deuteronomy that emphasize human responsibility and these are attractive to contemporary Christian thinkers trying to develop an 'ethics of the environment'. While the passages do not directly deal with environmental issues, they suggest that human beings should not destroy natural things without justification. Thus, when an army is besieging a city, it should not destroy trees: 'If you besiege a town for a long time, making war against it in order to take it, you must not destroy its trees by wielding an axe against them. Although you may take food from them, you must not cut them down. Are trees in the field human beings that they should come under siege from you? You may destroy only the trees that you know do not produce food; you may cut them down for use in building siege-works against the town that makes war with you, until it falls' (Deuteronomy 20.19–20).

GOING DEEPER

Roman Catholic teaching

For the past 30 years, the Roman Catholic Church has emphasized the need to protect the environment for the future of mankind. For example, Pope Paul VI wrote in 1971: 'Men are beginning to grasp . . . [that] the small delicate biosphere of the whole complex of all life on the earth [is] not infinite but, on the contrary, must be saved and preserved as a unique patrimony belonging to all mankind' (*Justice in the World*).

Pope John Paul II pointed to the 'suffering' of our planet: 'The profound sense that the earth is "suffering" is also shared by those who do not profess our faith in God. Indeed, the increasing devastation of the world of nature is apparent to all' (from 'The ecological crisis: a common responsibility').

Church of England teaching

Since 1970, the Church of England has emphasized environmental concerns in a series of reports: *Man in His Living Environment: An ethical assessment* (1970); *Our Responsibility for the Living Environment* (1986), and *Christians and the Environment* (1990).

A motion debated by the General Synod in July 1992 is typical of Anglican concern with 'stewardship' of the environment: 'This Synod, affirming its belief and trust in God the Father who made the world, believe[s] that the dominion given to human beings over the natural order is that of stewards who have to render an account.'

The debate: are threats to the environment exaggerated?

The optimists' view
Some writers claim calls for environmental protection have had an effect, although many problems remain. They also claim that

environmentalists have a vested interest in painting the darkest picture of the future of the environment because, by doing so, they will attract further government funds and voluntary donations.

For example, Bjørn Lomborg, a Danish academic, argues in his book *The Skeptical Environmentalist* (2001) that there are many indications that the condition of our rivers, seas, rain and atmosphere are improving.

He also argues that the world's forests are not diminishing overall, even though the sort of trees that they consist of might be changing. Since 1945, according to United Nations figures, the world's forests have utilized a steady 30 per cent of the planet's surface area. Forests in temperate areas have actually increased in the past 40 years. Tropical forests provide a partial exception – the Amazon forest has shrunk by 15 per cent – but their decline is slow.

The pessimists' view
Many people cannot see the contradictions in their behaviour towards the environment and, until they do, the environment will not be safe, the pessimists claim.

People might be committed to recycling but they also use their cars for very short trips, when walking would be adequate. Or, they seek out energy-efficient fridges and then fly halfway across the world on a package holiday.

The world's greatest polluter is the USA but it is also home to the world's most powerful environmentalist lobby (9 million Americans are members of environmental or conservation groups).

A significant cause of this contradiction might be that in crowded Europe it is easy to recognize environmental problems because they are very close at hand, while the vastness of North America allows people to ignore the effects of treating the environment badly.

Also, the USA is home to the headquarters of many of the world's most powerful corporations which, their critics claim, lobby to create a false picture to confuse the American public and the rest of the world.

Protecting the environment: environmentalist organizations

Many organizations have been founded in the past 50 years to protect the environment, of which Friends of the Earth and Greenpeace are prominent examples. (Fuller details of the activities of each organization can be found on its website.)

Cut the Carbon march, 14 July to 2 October 2007. In 18 marches held around the UK over an 80-day period, participants walked nearly 1,000 miles. The marches started in Bangor, Northern Ireland, and took in Edinburgh, Newcastle, Birmingham, Cardiff, the Labour Party Conference in Bournemouth and many other places along the way. Thousands of supporters joined the final leg from London Bridge to St Paul's Cathedral

Friends of the Earth (www.foe.co.uk)

Founded in 1969, Friends of the Earth is represented in 77 countries and has campaigned successfully for a ban on ozone-destroying CFCs, to reduce trade in rainforest timber and to increase support for cleaner energy technologies. It operates through groups linked together nationally and internationally.

Greenpeace (www.greenpeace.org.uk)

Founded in 1971, Greenpeace is a non-profit organization with a presence in 42 countries across Europe, the Americas, Asia and the Pacific. Among its objectives are:

- stopping climate change;
- protecting ancient forests;
- saving the oceans;
- ending whaling;
- stopping the nuclear threat;
- eliminating toxic chemicals;
- encouraging sustainable trade;
- preventing genetic engineering.

Society Religion and Technology Project (www.srtp.org.uk)

Founded in 1970, the Society Religion and Technology Project started with a major study on the environmental impact of North Sea oil and gas. It aims to develop a balanced and well-informed view of the issues. Although it has never adopted a specifically '**green**' agenda, it has often found much common ground with secular (non-religious) environmentalist organizations.

European Christian Environmental Network (www.ecen.org)

Inaugurated in 1998, the European Christian Environmental Network brings together representatives from the churches of 26 European countries, including Protestant, Anglican, Catholic and Orthodox traditions. It aims to help those working on environmental issues in the churches to share information, work better together and present a joint witness to the world.

Protecting the environment: what individuals can do

Individuals may feel that they can make little difference to the environment, but environmentalists argue that if enough individuals changed their habits of consumption, the environment would benefit.

Here are some important ares in which individuals can make a difference:

- saving energy in the home (setting heating thermostats lower, insulating houses better, solar panels);
- reducing the amount of energy used for transport (car pooling, using public transport, walking or cycling instead of driving for short journeys);
- recycling household goods (clothes, glass and newspaper banks);
- conservation work (clearing litter in your neighbourhood, helping with local land reclamation and improvement schemes).

Copyright © Shutterstock

Copyright © Shutterstock

SUMMARY

1 The landscape of Britain has changed vastly since the Industrial Revolution.

2 Since the nineteenth century, there have been attempts to protect places of natural beauty and buildings (e.g. formation and activities of the National Trust).

3 Attempts to protect the environment have grown since the 1970s (illustrated by the founding of environmentalist groups such as Greenpeace and Friends of the Earth).

4 Today, many threats to the environment have been identified.

   (a) The greenhouse effect, which changes the world's climate and increases the risk of flooding.

   (b) Depletion of the ozone layer, which reduces its filtering effect and exposes us to greater quantities of harmful radiation from the sun.

   (c) Deforestation, which aggravates the greenhouse effect and may reduce biodiversity.

   (d) Pollution, which comes from industrial and other waste spoiling the environment, e.g. acid rain caused by burning fossil fuels, agricultural run-off and household waste.

   (e) Nuclear waste, which can take centuries to become safe.

   (f) Rapid human population growth, which can lead to over-cultivation of land and water shortages, and threatens the survival of plant and animal species.

5 According to the Old Testament, God created the world but gave human beings dominion over it.

6 Some modern writers on the environment have seen the idea of dominion as a dangerous one that has encouraged human beings to see the earth as theirs to exploit.

7 Others argue that if ownership is not ultimately ours, our relationship to the world is one of stewardship. Thus we are accountable to God for our use of what has been given us.

8 Some of the rules in Deuteronomy for regulating Jewish life reinforce this view.

GOING DEEPER

9 The Christian churches stress stewardship and advise their members on how to fulfil their responsibilities towards the environment.

10 There is considerable debate over whether environmentalists have a vested interest in over-stating environmental risks to ensure support and donations. However, the world's largest economy, the USA, remains the world's greatest polluter and many people's personal behaviour is very inconsistent (e.g. supporting environmental causes while using forms of transport that waste fossil fuels).

11 Individuals might turn to organizations like Greenpeace, Friends of the Earth, etc., to put their environmentalist beliefs into action. They can also make personal efforts at energy conservation and at recycling household waste.

REVISION QUESTIONS

1 Name three threats to the environment. Explain in detail why one of these is a threat.

2 Define 'stewardship'.

3 Which passage in Deuteronomy can be used to suggest that we should respect the environment?

GOING DEEPER

4 Name one recent pope who has taught about the environment. Describe what he taught (be specific, quoting briefly).

5 Give one reason why concern for the environment might be exaggerated.

6 Give one reason why concern for the environment might *not* be exaggerated.

7 Name an environmentalist organization and *one* area of its work.

TOPIC
10

Suicide and euthanasia

Personal stories

Ben, a boy of 12, had been bullied at school. A week ago, he was caught by the police firing an air rifle at the window of a neighbour's house, to get even with one of the boys who had been bullying him at school. The police took him to the police station and cautioned him. The next day he hanged himself. His body was discovered by his younger sister, aged 10.

Glossary

euthanasia literally means 'dying well' and is the act of ending someone's life painlessly; the term is often used to mean 'medically assisted suicide'

hospice a place where you benefit from a range of services which offer dignity, peace, calm and freedom from pain at the end of life

living wills when people leave instructions not to be revived in certain circumstances (e.g. because of extensive brain damage), or for relatives, spouses or partners to be responsible for making decisions when they are unable to do so (e.g. when in comas)

morphine an opioid medication often used to relieve severe pain in cancer and some other diseases

palliative care provides relief from pain and other distressing symptoms for those who are dying

suicide the act of taking your own life

Simon was playing rugby one September afternoon. The pitch was still dry from a long, hot summer, and he fell badly when he was tackled. Something happened to his spine and he found he couldn't move. An ambulance was called and he was rushed to hospital. Emergency tests revealed that the damage to his spine was so great that he would be paralysed from the neck down for the rest of his life. Simon was conscious at this point. However, his breathing soon deteriorated rapidly and he was put on a respirator. He was also given heavy sedation.

Simon's parents were told that he had hardly any chance of escaping total paralysis. They told the doctors not to try any more to save Simon's life. The doctors were surprised but agreed to take Simon off antibiotics and sedate him more. Simon died the next day.

Copyright © Shutterstock

Discussion

- How do you react to true stories like Ben's? Can you imagine having a brother or sister who took his or her own life? If you knew someone as depressed as Ben, how would you try to help? In what ways was Ben's action wrong?

- If you had a horrible accident like Simon, would you want to die? Do you think that his parents had the right to make this decision? Did they do the right thing?

INTRODUCTION AND MAIN POINTS

'**Suicide is the most** common cause of death in men aged under 35. Men are nearly three times as likely to take their own lives than women.'

(BBC News; http://news.bbc.co.uk/1/hi/health/5079352.stm)

Suicide is surprisingly common. Far more boys and men than girls and women commit suicide. Those who have mental health problems or suffer from depression are the most likely to commit suicide. Teenagers – especially those who have issues with alcohol and drugs, are unhappy at school or in trouble with the law – are particularly at risk. Much older people, who have lost loved ones or friends, are also vulnerable. Their situation can be made worse by poor health and the loss of independence that ageing can bring. Those who attempt suicide once but are unsuccessful are at greater risk of trying again and being successful (one in ten teenagers who overdose will kill themselves within a few years).

Copyright © Shutterstock

Campaigns like 'Beatbullying' try to deal with bullying, which is a major problem in schools. A shocking number of young people attempt suicide as a result of bullying.

(www.beatbullying.org/dox/resources/statistics.html)

Suicide raises two principal issues:

1 how to help those at risk;

2 whether someone has the moral right to take his or her own life.

Related to suicide – and encompassing some of the same moral issues – is **euthanasia**, which can be defined as the act of ending someone's life painlessly. Euthanasia, when it is voluntary, is often called *assisted suicide*.

Suicide

Arguments in favour of suicide

The main argument in favour is that of choice. Humans have free will and suicide is an act that an individual is free to choose. In Ancient Rome and Ancient Greece, it was regarded as something that anyone was allowed to do. The tradition of seppuku (commonly known as hara-kiri) remains in Japan.

Other arguments in favour of suicide

- *Suicide is not necessarily due to mental illness.* It is, therefore, unsatisfactory to classify suicide and suicide attempts as signs of mental illness because they can be the free act of a sane person.

- *Suicide is not a crime.* Classifying suicide and suicide attempts as crimes (suicide was illegal in the UK until 1961) denies individual freedom. Also, if someone is suicidal because of mental illness, criminalizing his or her behaviour is not going to deter or help the person.

- *Suicide sometimes takes the form of self-sacrifice.* Many people admire those who sacrifice their lives for others (e.g. on the battlefield). Self-sacrifice, therefore, might be interpreted as a prime example of suicide as a positive choice.

Arguments against suicide

- Life is sacred and therefore we do not have the right to take it, whether it is someone else's life or our own.

- If you believe that life comes from God, suicide is the rejection of God's gift of life (an argument similar to the 'life is sacred' one; see page 116).

- Suicide is selfish because the person committing suicide ultimately disregards the pain and suffering that it will cause other people.

- Those who commit suicide ignore the possibility that circumstances might change and improve.

A compassionate response

Whatever the issues surrounding suicide, many people react with compassion and concern because they recognize that those who attempt to kill themselves might be suffering from depression or some form of mental illness. Moreover, many suicide attempts are designed to attract attention and help rather than with the serious intention of ending a person's life.

In the early 1950s, Chad Varah, a vicar working in central London, established an emergency service for people who were in despair or feeling suicidal. The inspiration for this service came from Chad's own experience. He had conducted a funeral for a 15-year-old girl who had committed suicide because she thought that she had contracted a sexually transmitted disease when, in fact, she was menstruating (having her period).

> **'Chad's belief was** the same as those of Samaritans today: that by listening to someone's problems and offering them the time and space to work things through, they may be able to find the strength to find a way forward.'
>
> (www.samaritans.org)

Copyright © Shutterstock

Chad initially set up a drop-in service with a telephone line for those who could not visit in person. The demand for the service grew so much that he began to recruit volunteers to help him. The resulting organization, founded in 1953, was called Samaritans (www.samaritans.org).

The Samaritans select and train volunteers to answer telephone calls from those in despair and feeling suicidal. The volunteers are unpaid and provide a 24-hour service. Although many of the volunteers are Christians they are not allowed to promote their religious beliefs in this context. Today there are over 200 Samaritans branches throughout the UK and thousands of volunteers.

Euthanasia

Medicine has made very great advances in recent decades. For instance, in ages past, babies born very prematurely would often die, whereas today many can survive, although sometimes with an inferior quality of life. Modern medicine has also made it possible for many people to live to a very advanced age but sometimes with a much diminished quality of life. However, despite the advances that medicine has made, there

Presumption in favour of prolonging life

'Following established ethical and legal (including human rights) principles, decisions concerning potentially life-prolonging treatment must not be motivated by a desire to bring about the patient's death, and must start from a presumption in favour of prolonging life. This presumption will normally require you to take all reasonable steps to prolong a patient's life. However, there is no absolute obligation to prolong life irrespective of the consequences for the patient, and irrespective of the patient's views, if they are known or can be found out.'

(General Medical Council, 'End of life care'; www.gmc-uk.org)

are still conditions, such as multiple sclerosis or muscular dystrophy, which are incurable and which can lead to a very low quality of life and a total dependence on others.

These circumstances make some people want to intervene to give the person with a very low quality of life the possibility of a 'gentle

'Palliative care for adults:

- provides relief from pain and other distressing symptoms;
- affirms life and regards dying as a normal process;
- intends neither to hasten nor postpone death;
- integrates the psychological and spiritual aspects of patient care;
- offers a support system to help patients live as actively as possible until death;
- offers a support system to help the family cope during the patient's illness and in their own bereavement;
- uses a team approach to address the needs of patients and their families, including bereavement counselling, if indicated;
- will enhance quality of life, and may also positively influence the course of an illness;
- is applicable early in the course of illness, in conjunction with other therapies that are intended to prolong life, such as chemotherapy or radiation therapy, and includes those investigations needed to better understand and manage distressing clinical complications.'

(World Health Organization (WHO) definition of palliative care; www.who.int/cancer/palliative/definition/en/)

and easy death', i.e. euthanasia (derived from Greek words that mean 'dying well'). Here are a number of examples of why someone might have a poor quality of life:

- an injury that results in, for example, severe brain damage or almost total paralysis;
- a progressive, incurable and debilitating illness, such as multiple sclerosis;
- severe, uncontrollable pain (because of illness or injury) that will never improve or that might increase;
- an illness that will result in a slow and painful death, such as an aggressive cancer;
- an inability for the individual to care for himself or herself, owing to great age or dementia.

Euthanasia and palliative care

To help someone experience a 'gentle and easy death' is illegal in most countries of the world. However, when no more can be done for a patient, doctors switch from trying to save someone's life to giving him or her **palliative care** – that is, making the individual comfortable as he or she dies. Doctors might also let someone die by withdrawing or withholding treatment, or by giving treatment that can have the indirect effect of hastening death. To understand how this range of possibilities works, look at the table called 'Different ways of describing euthanasia' overleaf (see also 'Euthanasia: areas of confusion', page 118).

Argument in favour of euthanasia

A common view is that, in a free society, individuals can behave as they wish provided their behaviour does not interfere with the freedom of others. For example, you should be free to be a vegetarian, eat fast food or live where you want to. This freedom should extend – so supporters of euthanasia argue – to being able to decide when your life ends.

Different ways of describing euthanasia

Type	Definition	Example
Voluntary euthanasia, 'assisted suicide'	The person *wants* to die and asks for help, either because she can no longer take her own life, or fears that she cannot do so painlessly. Voluntary euthanasia is illegal in the UK but permitted in some countries, e.g. the Netherlands.	Someone with an incurable and incapacitating illness seeks help with dying, e.g. through a euthanasia clinic such as Dignitas in Switzerland.
Involuntary euthanasia	The person is *competent* to decide but makes no request to die. Involuntary euthanasia is often within the law or there is no prosecution following it.	An extreme case could occur on a battlefield. A soldier sees another terribly injured soldier dying in great pain, with no possibility of medical help. The first soldier does not enter into a discussion with the second mortally wounded soldier but shoots him to end his suffering. (Prosecution would be most unlikely.) A doctor has a patient who will not accept the fact of her imminent death. The patient does not give consent to euthanasia, but the doctor still withdraws the medication that would have prolonged her life. (This action is within the limits of normal, legal medical practice.)
Non-voluntary euthanasia	The person is *incompetent* to decide.	Doctors decide to turn off life support when someone is in a coma and brain dead; or an infant is born with no chance of survival and is allowed to die rather than receive treatment that might prolong life for a few hours. (This action is within the limits of normal, legal medical practice.)
Indirect euthanasia (also known as the 'law of double effect')	The provision of medication in amounts that hasten death. Indirect euthanasia is legal if killing is not the *primary* intention. (There is no question of its legality as long as there was no direct intention to kill.) However, if the doctor knows of the secondary effect, there may be doubt about whether he intended to end life just as much as he intended to relieve suffering. In which case, can ending life really be called a secondary (double) effect?	A patient is in the final stages of a fatal illness, drifting in and out of consciousness. He can no longer swallow liquids and appears to be in distress. The doctor gives him a large dose of **morphine** which calms the patient but also hastens his death. A person is in the final stages of a fatal illness and is fully alert but entirely dependent upon carers for all her bodily needs, which is distressing to her since she feels it deprives her of dignity. Her pain is well managed with modest pain relief. The doctor increases the pain relief knowing that it will probably shorten her life. He can claim he is doing so to relieve pain but privately believes that the person will be spared continuing indignity.
Passive euthanasia	*Passive* euthanasia occurs when the doctor's primary concern is to relieve pain. He can be said to be *passive* about whether this treatment hastens death or not.	A person is still conscious but distressed. The doctor increases the pain relief to calm the patient who then loses consciousness and dies shortly afterwards – more quickly than if the pain relief had not been increased.
Active euthanasia	Specific actions are required, i.e. administering drugs to bring about death, which is illegal in the UK but not in some other countries, such as the Netherlands.	A doctor gives medication, in a quantity she knows will kill, to a person with a fatal illness and a very poor quality of life.
Passive or active?	A grey area exists where treatment or nourishment is withdrawn. The intention is not to 'strive officiously to keep alive', which many would regard as compassionate. The question remains whether withdrawing treatment or nourishment is 'letting nature takes its course' – a passive approach – or acting to shorten life – an active approach. The governing body for doctors, the General Medical Council (GMC), has issued guidelines for doctors to help them act ethically and legally in such cases.	A patient in a coma contracts pneumonia, which could be treated with antibiotics. Since treatment would prolong the patient's dying, antibiotics are not given and no attempt is made to hydrate (give liquids to) her. A person is suffering from the final stages of dementia and is also suffering from heart failure. The doctor marks the medical records 'Do Not Attempt Cardio-Pulmonary Resuscitation' (DNACPR). If the person were to have a heart attack, there would be a likelihood of further loss of mental function (through interruption of oxygen to the brain) for a person already severely debilitated.

They also believe that doctors should be allowed to assist people who either cannot carry out euthanasia by themselves or believe they can die painlessly only with medical assistance. To further support this argument, those in favour of euthanasia point to the fact that suicide became a right when it was decriminalized in the UK in 1961.

Here are two reasons why some people might choose voluntary euthanasia.

1 *Incurable and terminal illness.* Some illnesses, e.g. muscular dystrophy, are very difficult to offer good palliative care for. Some people feel that they, or their relatives, do not want to live in constant pain and that if there is no effective treatment then euthanasia should be an option.

2 *Poor quality of life.* If the quality of your life has become very poor – either because you are living in constant pain or you are completely dependent upon the care of others – you should be allowed to end your life if you wish.

Arguments against euthanasia

- Taking one's own life is not something that can be done in isolation. Other people will always be affected: your family, friends and those who provide medical care.

- From a Christian point of view, life is a gift from God and something sacred. We do not, therefore, have the right to take our own lives. However, Christians also believe in forgiveness and trust that a loving, merciful God might forgive those who commit suicide (and, by extension, euthanasia). But this view does not mean that suicide and euthanasia are 'right', merely that they might be forgivable.

- There is a risk that if euthanasia were legalized, it would become widespread. For example, when abortion was legalized in 1967, it was meant to be available only as a last resort. But since then, abortion has virtually become available on demand. Therefore, legalizing euthanasia might have a similar result – it might become easily and readily available.

- The cost of health care might cause people to think of legalized euthanasia as a cheaper – and therefore acceptable – alternative to expensive treatment and care when there is little or no prospect of recovery for the patient.

- The families of the very sick and dependent might also find euthanasia an attractive choice since they would be freed of the burden of caring. This option might lead to families bringing undue pressure to bear on their sick relatives to ask for euthanasia.

- People who make **living wills** might find themselves vulnerable to compulsory euthanasia. Once they had expressed the wish that doctors should not revive them or strive to keep them alive if they become very ill, there is the risk that their doctors and relatives might be quick to opt for euthanasia.

- Serious illness can affect people's moods. On one day, someone might want to die but, on another, he or she might want to live. If euthanasia were readily available, it might be given before the individual could change his or her mind.

- To expect doctors to assist people to die is contrary to the basic principles of their profession, which are to treat illness and save lives. To legalize euthanasia would modify these principles and potentially change the relationship between patients, doctors and patients' relatives, which might undermine public trust in the medical profession.

- Permitting euthanasia might deny people the chance to prepare for death, and their relatives the opportunity to prepare for their loved one's death.

✺ GOING DEEPER

Self-sacrifice and suicide

Many people have given their lives to save others. The sacrifice of Father Maximilian Kolbe (1894–1941) is a striking example. Before the Second World War, he founded Franciscan friaries (communities for friars) in his native Poland and elsewhere.

When Poland was invaded by the Germans, Fr Kolbe sent most of the friars home from the friary. He and a few remaining friars turned the friary into a shelter for 3,000 refugees, including 2,000 Jews. The friary came under suspicion and was closed down in 1941. Fr Kolbe was arrested and taken to Auschwitz.

In July 1941, a man escaped from the bunker where Fr Kolbe was held. The Germans had a rule that they would execute ten men for every one that escaped. So, ten were chosen, including Franciszek Gajowniczek, imprisoned for helping the Polish Resistance. He cried out in anguish, wondering what his wife and children would do without him. Fr Kolbe stepped forward and said to the camp commandant: 'I am a Catholic priest. Let me take his place. I am old. He has a wife and children.' The commandant could not believe what he had heard and asked Fr Kolbe to repeat what he had said, which he did. The commandant gave in to the request.

Fr Kolbe was thrown down the stairs of Building 13 together with the other victims, and left to die without food or water. Hunger and thirst soon overcame the ten. Fr Kolbe 'encouraged the others with prayers, psalms, and meditations on the Passion of Christ. After two weeks, only four were alive. The cell was needed for more victims, and the camp executioner, a common criminal called Bock, came in and injected a lethal dose of carbolic acid into the left arm of each of the four dying men. Kolbe was the only one still fully conscious and, with a prayer on his lips, the last prisoner to raise his arm for the executioner. His wait was over' (www.fatherkolbe.com).

Fr Kolbe was made a saint in 1981. Franciszek Gajowniczek, the man whose life he saved, died in 1995 at the age of 95. His wife had survived the war but his sons had been killed.

You might ask where the dividing line comes between Fr Kolbe's act and suicide. The difference must be one of intention. Suicide involves not wanting to live any longer and deliberately taking one's life. When a man or woman gives up his or her life for someone else, it is to preserve the other person's life, not because he or she wants to die. An act of this type is a self-sacrificial one. Christians would connect such behaviour with Jesus' offering his life for others and point to a saying of Jesus in John's Gospel: 'No one has greater love than this, to lay down one's life for one's friends' (John 15.13).

The gate of Auschwitz, bearing the words *Arbeit macht frei* ('Work sets you free'), viewed from inside the notorious Nazi concentration camp

The crematorium in Auschwitz

Euthanasia: areas of confusion

When a patient's quality of life is poor and death is imminent, the focus of medical care shifts from sustaining life and restoring health to aiding the person towards a dignified death.

The law of double effect (indirect euthanasia)

Sometimes, when a patient dies under medical supervision, it is not clear whether the death was intended. For example, doctors might administer morphine to control pain in some cases of terminal illness. The primary purpose of increasing the morphine dose is to reduce suffering – it is palliative – but its secondary effect is to shorten life. This consequence is called the *law of double effect*. Such treatment happens daily in hospitals and when people are dying at home. It is not regarded as illegal and is an example of normal medical practice. (It is also called *indirect euthanasia*.)

Some critics point out that, although the primary intention is for the treatment to make a dying person comfortable, the doctor administering it also knows that it will shorten life. The doctor, therefore, could be said to have intended the patient's death, i.e. that he or she should receive euthanasia. On the other hand, indirect euthanasia is not the same as administering a drug that causes only death and has no other effect.

Withdrawing or withholding treatment

Doctors may also shorten life by withdrawing treatment. For instance, doctors might decide to turn off the life-support system that is keeping alive someone in a permanent vegetative state (PVS). This act would result in the PVS patient dying of natural causes shortly afterwards. Such a decision could be controversial because there have been cases where PVS patients have recovered, even after years in a coma.

It is also legitimate medical practice to advise against an operation or treatment that would give the patient a few more weeks of life when it might serve only to prolong distress and suffering. For example, if a person is already severely debilitated by general ill health, he or she may choose not to be treated for life-threatening pneumonia.

Living wills

The Mental Capacity Act, which came into operation in 2007, allows people to make living wills. In a living will, someone can – years in advance – make it clear how they want doctors to act in the event of an illness that renders them incapable of deciding for themselves. They might, for instance, demand that life-preserving treatment be withdrawn if they become too sick to communicate or to feed themselves. Life-preserving 'treatment' here could include being given food or drink. Critics of this new law have described it as euthanasia by the back door.

Hospices

The first modern **hospice**, St Christopher's, in south London, was opened in 1967. Since its opening, a worldwide hospice movement has grown that has fundamentally changed the way that we approach death and dying.

Hospice or palliative care aims to transform the experience of dying. The basic idea of hospice care is that dying is a natural part of life. Hospices try to care for the physical, emotional, social and spiritual needs of people approaching the end of life. They aim to offer dignity, peace, calm and freedom from pain. To achieve this goal, hospices have multidisciplinary teams that provide a range of services: pain control, symptom relief, skilled nursing care, counselling, complementary therapies, spiritual care, art, music, physiotherapy, reminiscence, beauty treatments and bereavement support.

A therapy dog with a hospice patient

SUMMARY

1 Suicide is surprisingly common. Far more boys and men take their own lives than girls and women.

2 The age groups most at risk are teenagers and old people. Those with mental health problems or depression are also at risk.

3 Suicide raises two principal issues: how to help and whether individuals have the right to take their own lives.

4 Arguments in favour of suicide:

(a) Suicide is an act that people are free to choose.

(b) Suicide should not necessarily be seen as sign of mental illness – a sane person might choose suicide as an act of free will.

(c) Suicide is not a crime.

(d) Suicide can be an act of self-sacrifice to benefit others.

5 Arguments against suicide:

(a) Life is sacred and no one has the right to take it.

(b) For those who believe life derives from God, suicide is a rejection of his gift.

(c) Suicide is selfish because it disregards the suffering caused to others.

(d) Those who commit suicide ignore the possibility that circumstances might improve.

6 Most people's reaction to suicide or suicide attempts – and to requests for euthanasia – is one of compassion.

7 Making compassionate provision for those thinking of suicide was Chad Varah's motive for founding the Samaritans in 1953.

8 Euthanasia means 'dying well'.

9 People seek euthanasia when their quality of life has become or seems about to become very poor.

10 There are different categories of euthanasia:

(a) voluntary euthanasia, 'assisted suicide'

(b) involuntary euthanasia

(c) non-voluntary euthanasia

(d) indirect euthanasia (the 'law of double effect').

11 A distinction can also be made between passive euthanasia and active euthanasia.

12 Arguments in favour of euthanasia:

(a) In a free society, people should be free to end their lives painlessly or have medical assistance to do so.

(b) Suicide (of which euthanasia is a form) was decriminalized in 1961.

(c) Some illnesses are not alleviated by palliative care.

(d) Some people's quality of life deteriorates so badly that choosing to end their lives should be permitted.

13 Arguments against euthanasia:

(a) Taking one's life affects many others.

(b) For Christians, life is sacred: no one has the right to take it.

(c) God may forgive those who commit euthanasia, although his willingness to forgive does not make euthanasia right.

(d) If legalized, euthanasia might become widespread.

(e) Legalized euthanasia might be seen as cheaper than expensive treatment.

(f) Families of the very sick might see euthanasia as an escape from the burden of care and push them to ask for euthanasia.

(g) Those who make living wills might find themselves vulnerable to compulsory euthanasia.

GOING DEEPER

14 Self-sacrifice differs from suicide in its intention.

15 Christians see self-sacrifice as modelled on Jesus' self-sacrifice, when he gave up his life for others.

16 The balance shifts from cure to helping the patient to die with dignity when quality of life is poor and death close. However, pain-relieving medication may have a double effect: relief of pain and hastening death.

17 When patients are in a permanent vegetative state (PVS), doctors might turn off life support. But to do so could be controversial because some PVS patients do recover.

18 Doctors may also withhold treatment or nourishment that might extend life from a dying patient because giving them could prolong suffering.

19 Living wills enable individuals to say how they want doctors to act in the event of an illness that renders them incapable of deciding for themselves. Critics of this provision have described it as euthanasia by the back door.

20 Hospice or palliative care aims to transform the experience of dying by caring for people's physical, emotional, social and spiritual needs as a whole.

REVISION QUESTIONS

1 Which groups of people are most likely to attempt or commit suicide?

2 How are suicide and euthanasia linked?

3 What is most people's first reaction to suicide?

4 Which organization was founded in 1953 to help those tempted to take their own lives?

5 Give a basic definition of euthanasia.

6 When might euthanasia be considered an option?

7 What is the difference between voluntary and involuntary euthanasia? Give an example of each.

8 What are the arguments for suicide as an acceptable individual choice?

9 What are the arguments against suicide as an acceptable moral choice?

10 What are the main arguments in favour of euthanasia?

11 What are the main arguments against euthanasia?

GOING DEEPER

12 What makes self-sacrifice different from suicide?

13 What becomes the focus of medical care when someone is dying?

14 Explain what is meant by the law of double effect.

Personal stories

Dylan is a Christian, but his friend Nick is not. One day, Nick suggests that they watch a film which Dylan has heard his parents, who are also Christian, call 'shameful' because of its irreverent portrayal of Jesus. Dylan does not want to disappoint Nick or to appear boring, but he is concerned that he will be upset by seeing the film and that in so doing he will offend God, so he tries to get out of watching it.

Isaac Hayes (1942–2008) provided the voice for the character Chef in *South Park*. He was happy to contribute to episodes of the TV series which satirized religions including Christianity, Islam and Judaism. But when the writers of the show turned to Hayes' own religion, Scientology, he objected, saying: 'There is a place in this world for satire, but there is a time when satire ends and intolerance and bigotry towards religious beliefs of others begins.' One of the show's writers, however, said that Hayes wanted a different standard for religions other than his own, adding: 'and, to me, that is where intolerance and bigotry begin'.

Discussion

- Should someone be offended at the unfavourable or offensive portrayal of his religion in the media?
- Is it right for a Christian to enjoy something that is blasphemous?
- Should a person's beliefs be protected (whether morally or legally) from ridicule by those who do not share those beliefs?
- Is it reasonable to apply a double standard, i.e. to tolerate people making fun of religion so long as it is not your own that is being mocked?

Glossary

blasphemy contemptuous speech, writing, or action concerning God or anything held as divine

censorship an action that limits freedom of speech for moral, military, political, religious or corporate reasons

democracy government by representatives elected by the people

Eastern bloc the group of eastern European states which came under the sway of communism under the Soviet Union (1922–91)

freedom of speech the freedom to express opinion in public speech or published form

Holocaust the killing of 6 million Jews and around 5 million others, including gypsies, political prisoners, disabled people and homosexuals, by the Nazis during the Second World War

lobbying the act of trying to influence the vote of someone in a position of power (e.g. a politician), often on behalf of an organization

propaganda information (which may or may not be true) presented in a limited and emotionally charged way to control public opinion

Power to the press

The Sun is read by approximately 7.5 million people every day. In the 1992 general election, the newspaper strongly opposed the Labour candidate, Neil Kinnock. Until the polling day itself, he was the favourite to win, but on the day of the election, *The Sun* ran the headline, 'If Kinnock wins today will the last person to leave Britain please turn out the lights'. The Conservative party gained a surprise victory, and the next day, *The Sun* proudly proclaimed, 'It's The Sun Wot Won It'. We shall never know whether there really was a straightforward cause-and-effect relationship, but the newspaper itself believed – and wanted its readers to be aware – that it could have tremendous influence on public opinion. (www.nmauk.co.uk)

INTRODUCTION AND MAIN POINTS

We base many of our own attitudes and beliefs on those of our friends and family, but the media also constantly influence us. Sometimes the media support government policy and act in the 'national interest' (e.g. by condemning an act of terrorism); sometimes they try to affect the way we think purely for their own ends (e.g. to make us buy a product).

Media

The word 'media' is the plural of the word 'medium', which means something through which something else is transmitted, e.g. sound is transmitted to our ears through the medium of air.

In our society, the plural form of the word is more commonly used. 'Media' has come to refer to any means by which information, ideas and opinions are transmitted. The variety is huge and includes TV, newspapers, radio, cinema, videos, DVDs, newspapers, magazines, advertisements, the Internet and computer games.

Copyright © Shutterstock

All media are subject to some degree of censorship, but in the UK our right to '**freedom of speech**' means that, in practice, the government suppresses only news stories that might be a threat to the safety of the country. This stance contrasts markedly with the policy of the communist government of China, which strictly controls what information can be viewed on the Internet.

In the UK, the historical linking of Church and State still gives Christians a privileged position with regard to what people say about their faith, despite the abolition of the laws on **blasphemy** (see page 132). However, mounting pressure from secular groups, as well as the increasingly multi-faith citizenship of our country, is eroding this preferential treatment.

Seeking and avoiding publicity

When politicians hope to be elected or companies try to sell a new product, they are eager for 'good media coverage'. They want to be seen on TV and written about favourably in the press.

On the other hand, politicians or celebrities who have done something embarrassing or illegal object to media interest and call it an invasion of privacy.

The influence of the media

There is considerable debate about how much the media affect the way we think and behave. Those who think that the media shape our lives point towards the way they can turn someone unknown into a celebrity overnight, and just as quickly destroy that person's reputation.

The celebrity Jade Goody is a good example of the media's power to make or break a reputation. After Jade died, the *Daily Telegraph* described how the media had treated her: 'The first time she was mentioned in the press, in May 2002, Jade Goody was described as a "pretty dental nurse, 20, from London". But 24 hours later, as she began her gobby, ignorant trajectory in the *Big Brother* house, *The People* went on the attack under the headline: "Why we must lob the gob". Before long, it was open season. *The Sun* called her a hippo, then a baboon, before launching its campaign to "vote out the pig". The *Sunday Mirror* rejected porcine comparisons on the grounds that it was "insulting – to pigs"' (22 March 2009).

However, it is not simply through making and destroying 'celebrities' that we feel the influence of the media. Every day we are bombarded with advertising; no one would bother to advertise unless they believed that it affected our behaviour. An American **lobbying** group – LimiTV – explains:

> Television, video games, popular music and other media are not simply harmless forms of entertainment. The media helps to shape attitudes and behaviors. TV advertisers, for example, are well aware that media shape attitudes about products and services. They pay handsomely for advertising opportunities and skillfully manipulate words and images to draw attention to their products.
> (www.limitv.org/literacy.htm)

On the other hand, many popular TV shows owe their popularity to the fact that they reflect our lives, or at least the situations that most people experience. Weddings, funerals and love affairs in the major 'soaps' (*EastEnders, Coronation Street, Emmerdale, Holby City*, etc.) attract large audiences.

News portrayals of Christianity

Christianity probably receives its widest exposure in the British tabloids.

Positive coverage

Some press coverage of Christianity can be very positive. For example, the Church of England nun, Sister Frances Dominica, who founded a hospice for children, Helen House in Oxford, receives this kind of coverage, as described in the box at the top of the next page.

Negative coverage

However, much of the media sets out to portray Christianity as out of touch, silly or scandalous. For example, see *The Sun*'s treatment of the Church of England's policy about tombstones and the way in which the debate about sexuality is reported in the two boxes at the bottom of the next page.

News portrayals of important religious figures

Important religious figures who receive the most media attention are principal church leaders, like the Pope and the Archbishop of Canterbury, and those whose work is remarkable, e.g. figures like Archbishop Desmond Tutu and Mother Teresa. Sometimes bishops who are outspoken or who do something foolish will receive publicity simply because of their office, e.g. a bishop who is drunk in public is more interesting to the press and public than a drunk footballer caught coming out of a

'Interview: Margarette Driscoll meets Sister Frances Dominica

Two men are walking along a beach covered in starfish washed up by the tide. The younger man picks one up to throw it back into the sea. The older one says: "Why bother? It won't make any difference; once the sun gets up they'll all be baked dry and die anyway." The young man looks down at the starfish he's holding. "It'll make a difference to this one," he says.

It is this little story, rather than any amount of high-flown Anglican theology, that has formed a guiding principle for Sister Frances Dominica, founder of Helen House, the world's first children's hospice. She recounts it as we are walking around the neighbouring Douglas House – opened by the Queen on Friday – the 29th hospice in a nationwide chain Sister Frances has created but in itself

another first, as it will provide care for terminally ill young adults.

Sister Frances is 61 and known to the families who use Helen House simply

Sister Frances Dominica with Jordi, a young friend who stayed in Helen House and Douglas House

as 'Frances'. Nobody talks about her without using the word 'inspirational' and millions were moved and enthralled when she appeared on *Desert Island Discs* recently. One colleague said she was driving and had to pull in to listen to the programme. Several others admitted it had made them cry.

For more than 20 years, Frances has been intimately involved with families whose children are terribly disabled or dying. She has comforted and held hands with people suffering the greatest pain life can dish out. Yet it has left her an optimist. She has a broad, warm smile for everyone and a calm, quietly authoritative way of speaking that you can see would be very reassuring in a crisis.'

(*Sunday Times*, 22 February 2004)

'Nicknames have been banned
from gravestones by the Church of England, it was revealed yesterday.

A ruling states a person's full name as it appears on their birth certificate must be engraved.

The decision emerged when a family appealed to church authorities because they were not allowed to use a shortened version of a dad's name.

Relatives of Rodney William Lawton Stone said he had never liked his full name and would have preferred just "Rod Stone" to mark his grave.

But clerical legal chiefs said no

exceptions should be made to the rule that full names are required on memorials.'

(*The Sun*, 2 July 2008; emphasis added)

'Outrage at gay vicars' "wedding"

A bishop ordered an inquiry last night after two gay vicars were the first homosexuals to be "married" in a church.

Christians were outraged when Anglican priests the Revd Peter Cowell and the Revd Dr David Lord took their vows and exchanged rings at a lavish ceremony.

The pair – wearing morning suits and joined by bridesmaids and their best men – walked to the altar amid a fanfare of trumpets and vowed to stay together "for better for worse, for richer for poorer".'

(*The Sun*, 16 June 2008)

nightclub. Also, people who campaign for something – e.g. restricting the sale of pornography – might attract more attention if they are known to be Christian.

Popes: John Paul II and Benedict XVI

John Paul II was the Pope for almost 27 years and received (and invited) enormous media attention. Much of this was favourable, especially in the early years of his papacy. However, when his conservative stance on the role of women in the Church, contraception and homosexuality became well known, the coverage was often critical. But towards the end of his life, his frailty and struggle with debilitating illness elicited sympathy. At his funeral, the crowd chanted '*Santo subito!*' ('Sainthood now!') and this event was widely and favourably reported.

Pope Benedict XVI, John Paul II's successor, has received a varied press. His international visits to Roman Catholics outside Italy are widely and generally positively reported. However, he has provoked controversy by speaking about Islam and visiting the Holy Land.

'**The Pope on Sunday** said he was deeply sorry Muslims had been offended by his use of a mediaeval quotation on Islam and violence, but his words failed to quell the fury of some Islamic groups demanding a full apology.'

(*Daily Mail*, 19 September 2006)

Rowan Williams, Archbishop of Canterbury

Dr Rowan Williams, Archbishop of Canterbury since 2003, initially received a very good press, but his period in office has been coloured by controversy within the worldwide Anglican Communion (a network of churches linked together by history and a connection with the office of the Archbishop of Canterbury). Some Christians within the Anglican Communion have a liberal attitude to issues such as the ordination of

homosexuals and women as priests and bishops; others resist this move as a deviation from traditional values. Dr Williams has been unable to please both groups and this has provoked critical press coverage.

Mother Teresa

Famous contemporary Christians like Mother Teresa continue to have an impact into old age and even after death. For her work among very poor people in Calcutta (Kolkata), Mother Teresa is portrayed as a great example

Copyright © Press Association

'**The squalid truth behind the legacy of Mother Teresa**

The nun adored by the Vatican ran a network of care homes where cruelty and neglect are routine. Donal MacIntyre gained secret access and witnessed at first hand the suffering of "rescued" orphans.

The dormitory held about 30 beds rammed in so close that there was hardly a breath of air between the bare metal frames. Apart from shrines and salutations to "Our Great Mother", the white walls were bare. The torch swept across the faces of children sleeping, screaming, laughing and sobbing, finally resting on the hunched figure of a boy in a white vest. Distressed, he rocked back and forth, his ankle tethered to his cot like a goat in a farmyard. This was the Daya Dan orphanage for children aged 6 months to 12 years, one of Mother Teresa's flagship homes in Kolkata. It was 7.30 in the evening, and outside the monsoon rains fell unremittingly.'

(*New Statesman*, 22 August 2005)

of Christian behaviour. However, there have also been some attempts to portray her unflatteringly.

Archbishop Desmond Tutu

Archbishop Desmond Tutu was one of the leading opponents of apartheid (the policy of keeping the races apart) in South Africa. He was the first black South African to lead the Anglican Church in South Africa, and he was awarded the Nobel Peace Prize in 1985 for his pursuit of a non-violent end to apartheid.

He has brought his great moral authority and charisma to many other causes. He headed South Africa's Truth and Reconciliation Commission, which investigated crimes committed by all the sides during the apartheid era. Tutu has also used his high profile to campaign against homophobia, poverty and racism, and to achieve an adequate response to AIDS. His courage and moral authority generally deter 'debunking' coverage.

> **'Homophobia is as unjust as that crime against humanity, apartheid**
> *By Desmond Tutu*
>
> A student once asked me if I could have one wish granted to reverse an injustice, what would it be? I had to ask for two. One is for world leaders to forgive the debts of developing nations which hold them in such thrall. The other is for the world to end the persecution of people because of their sexual orientation, which is every bit as unjust as that crime against humanity, apartheid.
>
> This is a matter of ordinary justice. We struggled against apartheid in South Africa, supported by people the world over, because black people were being blamed and made to suffer for something we could do nothing about – our very skins. It is the same with sexual orientation. It is a given. I could not have fought against the discrimination of apartheid and not also fight against the discrimination that homosexuals endure, even in our churches and faith groups.'
>
> (*The Times*, 1 July 2004)

Film portrayals of Christianity

Christianity as such was not portrayed in the earliest films based on the Bible. Huge box office success was achieved with films based on Old Testament subjects, for example Cecil B. De Mille's *The Ten Commandments*. Part of the reason for choosing to film the stories of the Old Testament is that they yield lots of action scenes. Also, Old Testament stories are often less well known in detail to the public, which allows directors greater artistic licence.

The first films to depict Christianity – in the 1950s – were versions of the traditional passion play (a play presenting the trial, suffering and death of Jesus), made essentially for church audiences. Later commercial films like *The Greatest Story Ever Told* and *King of Kings* failed at the box office. The films that were a success – for example, *The Robe* and *Ben-Hur* – were based on fictional stories rather than the Bible and placed Jesus at a distance from the main characters.

In recent years, however, *The Passion of the Christ*, directed by ardent Roman Catholic Mel Gibson, was released. It focuses on the final hours of Jesus' life, showing explicitly the meaning of Jesus' 'dying for our sins'

> **'[Mel Gibson's] version** of the Gospels is harrowingly violent; the final hour of *The Passion of the Christ* essentially consists of a man being beaten, tortured and killed in graphic and lingering detail. Once he is taken into custody, Jesus (Jim Caviezel) is cuffed and kicked and then, much more systematically, flogged, first with stiff canes and then with leather whips tipped with sharp stones and glass shards. By the time the crown of thorns is pounded on to his head and the cross loaded on to his shoulders, he is all but unrecognizable, a mass of flayed and bloody flesh, barely able to stand, moaning and howling in pain.'
>
> (*New York Times*, 25 February 2004)

(the central belief of Christianity that Jesus' death on the cross was a sacrifice required to cleanse humanity of its sins). Gibson intended this film to convert unbelievers and strengthen the faith of believers.

The Passion of the Christ was commended by Pope John Paul II and was very successful among traditional Roman Catholics and Evangelical Protestants. However, some critics thought that this approval by Christians involved double standards. They argued that Gibson's film portrayed just as much violence as Quentin Tarantino's films, which some Christians condemn for 'gratuitous violence'.

Controversial portrayals of Christianity and Jesus

Apart from those designed to convey Christianity, there have been a number of films which have stirred controversy about Christianity. Notable is *The Da Vinci Code*, a thriller based on the novel of the same name by Dan Brown. The plot hinges on the claim that, for centuries, the Knights Templar and the Priory of Sion have kept secret the fact that Jesus and Mary Magdalene had a child, and that the 'Holy Grail' (an English rendering of the French *Saint-Graal*, which, in turn, is supposedly derived from the medieval French '*sang real*', meaning 'royal blood') is really the bloodline that descends from Jesus and Mary Magdalene.

The film ends with the revelation that the body of Mary Magdalene is buried under the new part of the Louvre Museum in Paris and that her and Jesus' descendants are alive today. This 'fact' is potentially so dangerous to the authority of the Roman Catholic Church – which has always claimed that Jesus never married and had no descendants – that an assassin from Opus Dei (a real Roman Catholic organization) is systematically murdering those who know the secret. To those tempted to believe in the plot, the Roman Catholic Church is shown in a poor light.

Other films, such as *The Last Temptation of Christ*, have also been controversial. The plot of *The Last Temptation* is complex (see www.imdb.com/title/tt0095497/ for a detailed synopsis) but the part that fuelled the most controversy was the crucifixion scene. In this part of the film, Jesus is tempted – the last temptation – to imagine the married life that he could have had if he had denied his destiny as the Son of God. He hallucinates on the cross and imagines making love to Mary Magdalene, having a child and living an ordinary life. To many Christian critics – some of whom never actually saw the film – depicting Christ having a sexual relationship with a woman was blasphemous (see 'Blasphemy' on page 132 for more details on the concept of blasphemy).

Books focusing on religious themes

The Chronicles of Narnia

Some of the most widely read books focusing on religion are those by C. S. Lewis. Seven of these together are known as The Chronicles of Narnia, which remain popular with children and young people, and have been made into films. The stories feature witches, mythical creatures, talking animals, far-off worlds and magical spells. On the surface, these might not necessarily seem attractive to a Christian audience but the books are filled with biblical images. The hero in *The Lion, the Witch, and the Wardrobe* is a lion called Aslan (Jesus is called a lion in the last book of the New Testament (see Revelation 5.5)). Aslan dies instead of a sinner, rises from the dead and, in doing so, defeats an age-old curse (a parallel to Christ's death and resurrection). Some critics have remarked that Lewis, through choosing to represent Christ as a big lion, portrays Jesus as 'muscular' and forceful rather than as the gentle forgiving figure that others perceive in the Gospels.

His Dark Materials trilogy

Written two generations later, the books of Philip Pullman – particularly the trilogy His Dark Materials – have appealed to as large an audience as Lewis's books. However, Pullman is on record as saying: 'I'm trying to undermine the basis of Christian belief' (www.washingtonpost.com/ac2/wp-dyn/A23371-2001Feb18). On the other hand, he has, at other times, denied his previous statement, saying: 'I'm not in the business of offending people . . . [my] books uphold . . . values that I think are important, such as life is immensely valuable and this world is an extraordinarily beautiful place' (see source above).

However, critics like Peter Hitchens see His Dark Materials as a deliberate contradiction of Lewis's The Chronicles of Narnia, which fits Pullman's view that Lewis's books are Christian **propaganda** (www.guardian.co.uk/uk/2002/jun/03/gender.hayfestival2002).

The books of both Pullman and Lewis use religious allegory, parallel worlds and children coping with adult moral decisions that affect the fate of those worlds.

Some Christians have found Pullman's novels offensive but Rowan Williams, the Archbishop of Canterbury, has argued that Pullman's work stimulates discussion and might feature in religious education lessons in schools.

Christian use of the media

Limitations on Christian broadcasting and advertising

The UK is very different from the USA where there are over 1,600 Christian TV and radio channels. Here in the UK, the law prevents the Christian churches from portraying themselves directly through national broadcasting on terrestrial TV and national radio. They can only broadcast through satellite and cable TV (e.g. GOD TV), local radio and the Internet.

Some Christian initiatives like the Alpha course are advertised on hoardings, and some Christian groups publish their own magazines. There are also Christian newspapers like the *Catholic Herald* and the *Church Times*, but these reach only a relatively small audience.

Despite the restrictions on Christian broadcasting, the BBC and ITV are legally required to schedule a limited amount of religious programming, e.g. certain church services, 'Thought for the Day' in the *Today* programme on BBC Radio 4 (which is not exclusively Christian) and *Songs of Praise* on BBC1.

The aim of Christian use of the media

Media representation of Christianity in the UK mirrors the approach to religious education taken in schools: it investigates and provides information about Christianity rather than trying to persuade people to believe. If you go to the website of the BBC, the public service broadcaster in the UK, and type in 'Christianity', you will find references to many programmes on TV, radio and online about Christianity, including Christian customs, ethics and history.

Major denominations (the Roman Catholic Church, Church of England, Methodist Church, etc.) in the UK have websites that aim to provide information and education for church members and enquirers. The information offered might be practical (e.g. how to get married) or related to faith (e.g. how to pray). To get an idea of the huge variety of information and education offered, simply search online using the names of any of the major denominations (e.g. 'Methodist Church UK website').

Freedom of speech

Freedom of speech is one of the most important features of a country that calls itself a **democracy**, like the UK. There can be no true democracy without the freedom to debate and criticize ideas and policies. In the Cold War era, the Soviet Union and **Eastern bloc** countries severely restricted the expression of opinions that were at odds with the government's line, and there were no democratic elections. Similar circumstances prevail today in countries such as North Korea.

Freedom of speech means allowing individuals to express opinions that might be grossly offensive to others. For example, there are **Holocaust**-deniers who deny the extent of the Holocaust (Holocaust denial is a crime in some EU member states). The vast majority of people living in the UK know this opinion to be false and find it offensive, but if a society upholds free speech, it has to tolerate the expression of such opinions.

Censorship

However, tolerating different opinions does not mean that there is absolutely no limit to free speech. There are times when the right to say or do what you like is curtailed – or censored. Free speech can be censored to safeguard the rights of others, to protect society's values or the nation's security, or to protect vulnerable people from exposure to material considered harmful or offensive.

Wartime censorship

What we say and write might have to be censored in times of war. Governments restrict the publication of information that could assist the enemy. For example, precise information about the D-Day landings in

'How do I get married in the Catholic Church?

You and your fiancé(e) should go and see your parish priest as soon as you have decided to get married. Make sure that both he and the church are available to you before confirming your venue for the wedding reception, etc. If you intend to invite someone else to officiate at the ceremony (such as a relative or family friend who is a Catholic priest or deacon), then you must obtain permission for this also. Normally, at least six months notice is required.'

(http://catholic-ew.org.uk/Catholic-Church/Home-Mission/How-do-I/Get-married-in-the-Catholic-Church)

'Learn to pray

Much of the prayer of the Church of England is corporate, that is to say we do it together. [For example, the Anglican Church's Morning Prayer or Evening Prayer is said in churches all over the country at similar times.] Yet there is another side to our prayer life, our own individual prayers, as we try to share in Christ's prayer to his Father, that his will be done, his kingdom come.

The advice we provide here was originally written for a children's book. However, whether you are a child, young person or an adult, prayer is easier than you might imagine! Millions of people of every age pray every day.

You don't have to know any prayers if you want to pray – in fact, words can often get in the way. Picture Jesus, and then say what is in your heart, what you feel.

Remember! God hears every prayer – but not all prayers are answered in the way we might expect or desire: we don't always pray for his will to be done!'

(www.churchofengland.org/prayer-worship/learnpray.aspx)

Censorship aims to limit freedom of speech. It can be exercised by governments, companies, organizations or individuals. Censorship can operate in various areas: moral, military, political, religious, corporate and internet use.

- *Moral*: child pornography is censored by many countries because of the harm it does to the children exploited to produce it, and the behaviour that it might incite.

- *Military*: military authorities, especially in war time, will try to limit the publishing of information that might benefit the enemy. They might also try to censor information that could cause an adverse political reaction.

- *Political*: authoritarian governments censor information to control their populations and to prevent rebellion.

- *Religious*: powerful religious authorities might censor information they regard as objectionable or to limit the freedom of rival religions or denominations.

- *Corporate*: powerful media groups can censor what they publish or broadcast by excluding information or opinions conflicting with their corporate editorial line.

- *Internet*: the Internet has made borders between countries invisible and created difficulties for governments that want to control the free flow of information. Although governments cannot control the content of websites, they might try to control access to them by operating filters. Schools, universities and companies might also filter access to websites, so that users cannot entertain themselves during working hours or – in schools, particularly – access adult-rated sites.

1944 was not published at the time because it would have assisted the Germans' counter-attack. In recent conflicts, journalists 'embedded' with troops (so that they can report from the heart of the fighting) might censor their reports to some extent to protect the lives of those with whom they are living.

Censoring discriminatory views

There are also laws against discrimination 'on the grounds of religion or belief or sexual orientation' (Equality Act 2006). These laws mean that organizations and individuals must exercise care in what they say or publish about religion or belief. The Equality and Human Rights Commission is a body set up by the government to ensure compliance with these laws, which were first passed in the 1970s. For more on this subject, see Topic 5, 'Prejudice and discrimination', page 58.

Film classifications

The British Board of Film Classification (BBFC) rates films, DVDs and games to restrict which people see them. They range from 'U', universal or suitable for all, to 'R18', to be shown only in specially licensed cinemas. Some films, DVDs and games have parts taken out of them ('cuts') to allow them to receive a particular certificate.

These are the BBFC certificates:

- U: Universal – a film, DVD or game that is suitable for people aged 4 years and over; there will be very little in the nature of bad language, sex or violence, and what there is will be very mild.

- PG: Parental Guidance – this certificate indicates that the film, DVD or game might not be suitable for children under 8 years; parents are responsible for assessing whether the content is likely to upset their children. There might be mild bad language and mild references to sex and violence.

- 12/12A: Films, DVDs or games that may be seen by or sold to those aged 12 and over. 12A films may be seen by children under 12 if they are accompanied by an adult. The films, etc., might have mature themes, but strong language must be infrequent and violence must not dwell on detail.

- 15: No one under 15 is allowed to see a film or rent or buy a DVD or video game with this certificate. The strongest language is allowed if brief or justified; sex must not be detailed; violence must not dwell on pain.

- 18: No one under 18 is allowed to see a film or rent or buy a DVD or video game with this certificate. It must not risk harm to individuals, eroticize sexual assault or be a sex work.

- R18: Restricted – these products are available only in private clubs or sex shops. This certificate covers films with clear images of real sex.

THE CHRISTIAN VIEW

The media

For Christians, the media have both positive and negative aspects. On the one hand, the media broadcast informative programmes about Christianity, at home and abroad. Even in countries such as Iran where Christian missionaries are banned from teaching, satellite TV broadcasts enable them to reach more people than would otherwise be possible. On the other hand, some Christians believe that moral standards have declined as a result of the portrayal of 'immoral' behaviour in the media. They also think that their religion is too often treated disrespectfully by the media.

The portrayal of sex and violence

For many Christians, society's existing limitations on the portrayal of violence and sex are not strict enough. For example, in 2007 the General Synod of the Church of England debated the effect of further liberalizing the rating of films that contained sex and violence.

At the Synod, a Church of England priest, the Revd Richard Moy, argued that pornography has an effect on people's behaviour. He said: 'There have been numerous cases where defence barristers have asked judges to consider in mitigation that the defendant's actions were influenced by watching pornography' (www.thisislondon. co.uk/news/article-23387399-film-sex-and-violence-fatally-eroding-society.do). But this knowledge has had no effect on the BBFC, which continues to allow films that would once have been classified as R18 to be released with 18 certificates, and those once rated 18 to receive 15 certificates.

'**The Church of England yesterday warned** that the spread of hard-core sex and violence in films is "fatally eroding" standards of behaviour.

It questioned the increasingly liberal decisions by film censors and accused them of allowing wider and younger audiences to see pornography and violence.

The Church called for new thinking "about the effects of negative and degrading images on public safety".

The concern about the effects of films, DVDs and TV comes at the same time as growing fears over violence among the young – highlighted by a series of gun murders.

The attempt to put pressure on film censors and broadcasters at the Church's parliament, the General Synod, follows efforts by senior bishops to defend marriage and to do more to uphold Christian beliefs.

The Synod heard that "standards of human behaviour are being fatally eroded by constant subjection to suggestions and images promoting the exploitation of other human beings".'

(*London Evening Standard*, 2 March 2007)

The Synod also criticized programmes that mocked or humiliated people, giving as examples the *Little Britain* character Vicky Pollard – for mocking the speech of some teenage girls – and the show *Big Brother* for its apparent message that abusing and bullying people is acceptable as long as you are not racist (see source on previous page).

The main objections that the Synod had to the portrayal of violence and sex in films were the treatment of people as objects and the encouragement of anti-social behaviour. These attitudes are at odds with Christian teachings that every human being is uniquely valuable in the sight of God, to love your neighbour and treat the body as the temple of the Spirit. The Synod voted unanimously to condemn the exploitation of 'the humiliation of human beings for public entertainment' (see source on previous page).

GOING DEEPER

Blasphemy

Christian faith used to be central to the life of society, so blasphemy (expressing contempt for God) was seen as expressing contempt for society's values and something that threatened society. However, as Christianity became less central to the life of society, the concept of blasphemy was marginalized.

The last public prosecution for blasphemy was in 1922, when John William Gott was sentenced to nine months' hard labour for comparing Jesus to a circus clown.

In recent times, reference to the law of blasphemy was made by those British Muslims who wanted Salman Rushdie prosecuted for publishing *The Satanic Verses*, which they considered blasphemous.

Muslims were, however, unable to use the

blasphemy law as the basis for a prosecution because it did not cover Islam. As a result of an 1838 legal case, the offence of blasphemy only covered attacking the 'tenets and beliefs of the Church of England'. This view reflected the dominant position of the Church of England in the first part of the nineteenth century. Roman Catholics and Nonconformists (Baptists, Congregationalists, etc.) were not protected in the same way.

The fact that other Christian denominations and other faiths were not covered by the law of blasphemy was one of the reasons for the repeated calls for its repeal; it also seemed to be at odds with the European Convention on Human Rights (incorporated in UK law), which guarantees freedom of speech.

The law against blasphemy was finally repealed in 2008.

SUMMARY

1   The media constantly influence our attitudes and beliefs.

2   Advertising is an important function of the media.

3   All media are subject to some degree of censorship, although, in the UK and other democracies, it might be limited by the idea of 'freedom of speech'.

4   The way that someone is portrayed in the media is an important factor in determining how that person is perceived by the general public. Many would agree that someone's public image can be changed virtually overnight by the media.

5   The Church is often portrayed by the media as being out of touch or silly. The provocative or tactless remarks of a high-up figure in the Church, such as the Archbishop of Canterbury or the Pope, are particularly likely to attract media attention. Even Christians who have won widespread admiration, such as Mother Teresa, are occasionally criticized by journalists.

6   Films that focus on Christian themes are usually popular only if they include action scenes or violence, or if they distance themselves from the figure of Christ. Although Pope John Paul II commended *The Passion of the Christ*, critics claimed that it contained gratuitous violence. Other films, such as *The Da Vinci Code* and *The Last Temptation of Christ*, seem to set out to be deliberately controversial and to offend Christians.

7   The Narnia books of C. S. Lewis are an allegorical account of Christianity, although some critics think that the imagery of a powerful lion (Aslan) is inappropriate for Jesus. By contrast, Philip Pullman's His Dark Materials trilogy is considered by many to be specifically anti-Christian.

8   In contrast with the situation in the USA, Christians in the UK are banned from broadcasting material with an evangelizing or informative intent on terrestrial channels. Exceptions include a limited amount of religious programming, such as *Songs of Praise*.

9   Christian organizations are, however, able to make use of other media, such as satellite and cable TV, local radio, print media and the Internet to provide information and educate.

10 Freedom of speech is fundamental to a democracy because it allows us to criticize the government's behaviour. It also means that we have to allow others to express opinions that we personally find offensive.

11 Despite this freedom, democratic societies are subject to censorship to protect the rights of the vulnerable, particularly with regard to discriminatory views and pornographic or violent material.

12 Censorship might also be used by a state to protect itself from an enemy, particularly during times of war.

13 For Christians, there are some positive aspects of the media, such as informative programmes that may encourage interest in the Christian faith.

14 Some Christians believe that people's behaviour is affected by over-exposure to sex and violence in films, so they think that stricter censorship is needed.

GOING DEEPER

15 The laws against blasphemy used to give special protection to the Christian Church in this country, a privileged position to which secularists and members of other faiths objected.

16 When Christianity was central to society's life, blasphemy was regarded as contempt for society's values, but the concept has become increasingly marginalized as Christianity's influence has dwindled.

17 The law covered only attacks on Church of England beliefs: Roman Catholics and Nonconformists were not covered, nor were other faiths.

18 This omission led to repeated calls for its repeal, as did its apparent conflict with the right to freedom of speech guaranteed by the European Convention on Human Rights.

19 It was repealed in 2008.

REVISION QUESTIONS

1 List the principal types of media.

2 Explain how one influential Christian figure is portrayed unfavourably by the media.

3 Explain how another influential Christian figure is portrayed favourably by the media.

4 How do Christians react to the portrayal of violence in the media?

5 'Christians should not object to people making fun of their religion in the media.' Do you agree with this opinion?

6 In what ways can freedom of speech be limited?

7 Do you think it is right that a private organization, such as a newspaper publisher, should determine the result of the general election?

8 Is it important to consider more than one point of view by exposing yourself to different types of media?

GOING DEEPER

9 What was the original basis for having a law of blasphemy?

10 What made the law of blasphemy appear to be poorly adapted to contemporary society in the period immediately before its repeal?

How do we make up our minds about moral questions?

Personal stories

An American Roman Catholic lives in a state that is having a vote about whether to bring back the death penalty. Personally, he believes that there might be some occasions when the death penalty would be justifiable (for example, when someone kills others through an act of terrorism). However, he knows that the Roman Catholic Church teaches that the death penalty is wrong.

A unit of the British Army is fighting overseas. A mortar shell explodes among them, killing 2 soldiers and injuring 20. Three of the injured have been mutilated so badly that they are unlikely to survive. Five others have severe injuries but they should survive provided that they are airlifted to hospital quickly. The remaining soldiers have minor injuries.

Jane, a teacher, has two children at school. One, Brian, has just started at secondary school. His sister, Gill, is in Year 3. Jane has recently discovered that she is pregnant again. She and her husband, Gordon, had not intended to have any more children and find it difficult to afford bringing up the two they already have. Jane wonders whether she should continue with the pregnancy. Neither Jane nor Gordon go to church or have any particular religious belief.

Discussion

- Which ethical approach is likely to govern the American Catholic's behaviour? Why?
- Which ethical approach is likely to govern the behaviour of the army medical team when they arrive on the scene? Why?
- Which ethical approach is likely to govern Jane and Gordon's behaviour? Why?

Glossary

altruism unselfish concern for the welfare of others

deontological describing an ethical approach based on duty or moral obligation (from the Greek word *deon*, meaning 'that which is binding')

egoism the pursuit of your own welfare as the basis of your actions

infallible without error; referring to the Roman Catholic teaching that the Pope can make infallible proclamations (proclamations without error) concerning 'faith and morals' as 'supreme pastor and teacher of all the faithful'

magisterium the sacred teaching authority 'entrusted to the bishops in communion with the successor of Peter, the Bishop of Rome' (*Catechism of the Catholic Church*, para. 85)

Second Vatican Council (Vatican II) an important council of Roman Catholic bishops, held from 1962 to 1965, which abandoned the universal use of Latin for church services and made many reforms; it has great teaching authority

triage a system for deciding which patients receive care first

utilitarianism the pursuit of maximum benefit (pleasure, happiness, ideals) for the majority (often summarized as 'the greatest good for the greatest number')

INTRODUCTION AND MAIN POINTS

We have to make decisions every day. They can be quite trivial: on a school day, you might ask yourself whether you are going to spend time on Facebook or do the work that you need to for the next day's lessons. Or your decisions might have an effect on your future: which GCSEs should you do? What A level choices should you make?

But these are not moral decisions, although you might argue that spending time on Facebook rather than getting on with your school work is a bad use of your time.

Moral decisions are ones that involve choosing between what is right and what is wrong: should I copy someone else's coursework? Should I have unprotected sex? Should I continue with this pregnancy? Should I fight for my country? Should we let John, who is in a persistent vegetative state, continue on life support?

Once we have identified what are specifically moral decisions, we might ask how we become equipped to make them. We might also want to analyse what we are doing when we make them.

Our earliest experiences of calling something right or wrong will be at home and later at school. Initially, parents and older relatives, like older siblings or grandparents, will influence us. Later, teachers, peer groups and the media will affect how we think.

Our peer groups will have a considerable impact: from them we could acquire racist, sexist or homophobic attitudes; or, if some of them are involved in petty crime like shoplifting, we might copy them.

By the time we are teenagers, we will have been told by others countless times 'do this' or 'don't do that', or 'we do this' or 'we don't do that'. And what was a matter of doing as we were told when we were small children will become something that we decide for ourselves. By our teenage years, we will have

made others' attitudes our own: we will have internalized them.

This internalizing is partly responsible for what we call our conscience, the ability to decide between right and wrong. However, conscience is not just internalizing what other people have told us; conscience also involves scrutinizing our internalized attitudes to decide whether they are right or wrong. For example, a young woman might have been conditioned by her upbringing to subordinate her wishes to those of her father. But she could, by using her reason, decide that this behaviour is wrong.

As our ability to scrutinize the way we have been conditioned by our upbringing develops – as our conscience develops – we will make use of one of several ethical approaches (or a combination of them). But we will not necessarily be aware of how or why we are doing so, which is why we study ethics. The study of ethics enables us to become more aware of how we think, of how our conscience is working.

Although the study of ethics covers a wide range of approaches, we can begin to understand how we, and those around us, are making moral decisions by knowing about these three approaches:

1 me first (**egoism**);
2 doing what helps the greatest number of people (**utilitarianism**);
3 doing what you believe you ought to do (religious authority).

Me first (egoism)

Many people put themselves first. They think that 'I' matters more than anyone else. Of course, they might not admit this belief to themselves and they might get very annoyed if others say to them: 'You're just thinking of yourself.'

There is a technical word for this approach: 'egoism', which, like lots of technical words, comes from Latin (the Latin word for 'I' is *ego*).

There is much about popular culture that could loosely be called egoist: books on how to improve your life, how to look better, how to be slimmer and how to improve your home. All of these are focused on the self and making life better for the self. The current prevalence of this attitude has led some sociologists to dub those now in their 30s and 40s the 'me-generation' for their self-absorbed love of buying and acquiring.

Coping with
Life's Challenges

Moving on from adversity

DR WINDY DRYDEN

However, when you look closely at the different forms of egoism, it is not always easy to say whether the egoist's actions appear more selfish than those of someone who thinks about others.

For instance, if you take no notice of other people's needs, they will not cooperate with you. Similarly, if you break all your promises when it is in your self-interest to do so, others might not take you at your word and might become hostile towards you. Therefore, you best serve your own interests by taking into account the needs of others (as long as they do the same in return). So, to an observer your behaviour – as an egoist – might seem similar to that of the person who puts others' interests first.

Doing what helps the greatest number of people (utilitarianism)

Some people put others before themselves. This attitude is called **altruism** (a word derived from the Latin *alteri huic*, meaning 'to this other'). One kind of altruism involves making decisions that will benefit the greatest number of people.

A vivid illustration of this type of altruism is the way the emergency services respond to a terrorist incident or doctors work to deal with casualties on a battlefield. To ensure that the greatest number of people are treated effectively, medical staff attach '**triage** tags' to the injured, classing them according to how much help they need or could benefit from. These tags are colour-coded:

- black – the dead or dying who are beyond help;
- red – those who will die if they don't receive immediate attention;
- yellow – those who can wait for treatment;
- green – those who are often described as 'walking wounded', who need only a little help.

The technical word for this approach – seeking the greatest benefit for the greatest number – is called utilitarianism (from *utilis*, Latin for 'useful': helping the greatest number can be seen as the most *useful* way of using resources).

'**It was Jadick's** first experience in battlefield triage – forget the mortally or lightly wounded, save the rest – a concept easier to philosophize about than to practice.'

(http://forums.military.com/eve/forums/a/ tpc/f/9751945704/m/2630019441001)

Doing what you believe you ought to do (religious authority)

Christians believe that the Bible or religious leaders (bishops, priests and ministers) have the authority to guide moral decisions. They also believe that they have a duty to follow that guidance. There are, however, differences between denominations about the degree to

Copyright © Press Association

Roman Catholics recognize the Pope as someone who teaches with authority. Not only that, they believe him to be **infallible** in matters of 'faith and morals', and this belief makes their duty to follow the Pope's teaching stronger. The teaching authority of the popes and the Roman Catholic Church is called the **magisterium**. In the past 40 years, the popes' teaching has included the condemnation of artificial means of birth control, the death penalty, certain wars, euthanasia and genetic research on 'spare' embryos.

Anglicans and Orthodox Christians do not recognize the teaching authority of just one person. Rather, their archbishops and bishops give guidance to church members on moral issues, which those members might choose to respect and act upon. Anglican and Orthodox Christians do not, however, regard this guidance as authoritative in the way that Roman Catholics regard the Pope's teaching.

Duty-based ethical approaches may be described as **deontological**.

which Christians will consider that authority binding. Also, an individual's conscience might affect whether he or she will follow the guidance or teaching.

GOING DEEPER

Christians vary in what they believe: traditions and denominations

The body of Christian believers is huge and varied. Like Islam, Hinduism and Judaism, Christianity is a 'religion' or 'faith'. Broadly speaking, the Christian religion is divided into three major traditions:

- Orthodox (also known as Eastern, Greek or Greco-Russian)
- Roman Catholic
- Protestant.

Within the Orthodox and Protestant traditions, there are a number of different churches or denominations. For example, the Coptic Church, Ethiopian Church and Greek

Orthodox Church belong to the Orthodox tradition, while the Baptist Church, Methodist Church, Church of England and many others are Protestant. The Roman Catholic Church may be described as either a tradition or a denomination.

The teachings of the denominations

Each denomination has distinctive teaching, which is publicly available. The Roman Catholic Church, for instance, has the *Catechism of the Catholic Church* (see page 89). Each church has a website which gives a summary of its basic teaching and links to more detailed explanations (see pages 128–9).

Of course, there is a great deal of overlap between denominations: all Christians are opposed to killing people, for instance. But there are also differences of organization and practice. The Church of Scotland permits second marriages, whereas the Roman Catholic Church does not (except when an annulment has been granted, see pages 52–3).

The basis of authority – the starting point for deciding belief and practice – varies according to denomination. The Roman Catholics appeal to the magisterium (teaching authority) of the Church and to moral law (see page 40), whereas Protestants appeal to Scripture (the Bible).

Variety within a denomination

Not only do belief and practice differ between denominations, there is also variety *within* each denomination. Some Roman Catholics ignore the Church's magisterium: although the Church forbids artificial birth control, for example, many Roman Catholics use it.

The Church of England embraces a notable variety of belief and practice. It has members (Evangelicals) who are close to Methodists and Baptists in their belief and practice. But it also has members (Anglo-Catholics) who are closer to Roman Catholic belief and practice. The reason for this diversity is that the Church of England is a church that has kept 'Catholic' order (there are bishops, priests and deacons) but which, in a sense, began during the Protestant Reformation in the sixteenth century. The term 'in a sense' is used because many Anglicans would say that the rejection of the Pope's authority in 1534 ended the Church of England's relationship with the Pope but not with its earlier, Catholic history.

Therefore, in the Church of England there are a wide variety of approaches to the authority of the Bible and tradition. Some conservative Evangelicals (i.e. the more Protestant wing of the Church of England) claim to interpret the Bible literally, appealing to 'proof texts'. But other, more liberal Anglicans will insist on taking the texts' historical context into account when interpreting them. For this reason, a conservative Evangelical might take Jesus' teaching forbidding divorce literally and reject any possibility of remarriage. Liberal Anglicans might argue that Jesus

> '**He said to them**, "Whoever divorces his wife and marries another commits adultery against her; and if she divorces her husband and marries another, she commits adultery."'
> (Mark 10.11–12)

taught against divorce to protect first-century women, but that women today do not need that kind of protection.

The differences are often between 'liberals' and 'conservatives' rather than between denominations

Exam questions often ask how Christians respond to a moral question. From this outline of the teachings of the different Christian denominations, you will see that you cannot generalize about them. Also, each denomination is made up of a spectrum of belief. The spectrum of Roman Catholic belief can overlap with the spectrum of Anglican belief. In fact, 'liberal' members of different denominations can often have more in common with each other than with 'conservative' members of their own denominations. Therefore, a liberal Roman Catholic might have more in common with a liberal Anglo-Catholic than with a conservative, traditionalist Roman Catholic. A conservative Evangelical Anglican might agree on many more issues with a Baptist than with a liberal Anglican. There are similar ranges of belief, from liberal to conservative, in Judaism and Islam.

Sanctity of life

'Sanctity of life' is the term Christians use to show that they regard life as precious and of the highest value. Such a belief is widely, if not universally, accepted. For example, Article 3 of the Universal Declaration of Human Rights (1948) declares that: 'Everyone has the right to life, liberty and security of person'.

The use of the word 'sanctity' (from *sanctus*, the Latin word for 'holy') should alert us to the fact that the roots of this idea are religious. For Christians, the concept of sanctity of life (holiness of life) finds its roots in the both the New and Old Testaments of the Bible.

Biblical and Christian sanctity-of-life texts

New Testament

Luke 12.6, 7: 'Are not five sparrows sold for two pennies? Yet not one of them is forgotten in God's sight . . . Do not be afraid; you are of more value than many sparrows.'

Old Testament

Genesis 1.27: 'So God created humankind in his image, in the image of God he created them; male and female he created them.'

Psalm 139.13, 15, 16: 'For it was you who formed my inward parts; you knit me together in my mother's womb . . . My frame was not hidden from you . . . In your book were written all the days that were formed for me, when none of them as yet existed.'

Exodus 20.13: 'You shall not kill' (the Sixth Commandment (NJB)).

Early Christian writing

Didache: 'You shall not kill by abortion the fruit of the womb and you shall not murder the infant already born.'

New Testament

The example from Luke's Gospel (Luke 12.6–7, see the 'Biblical and Christian sanctity-of-life texts' box) shows that God places exceptional value on human life. After all, if every little bird counts in God's sight, imagine how much more he values every human life.

Old Testament

The New Testament teaching above can be seen as a development of Old Testament teaching. The first chapter of Genesis singles human beings out as particularly valuable (see Genesis 1.27). If human beings are made in the image of God, they are more valuable than other creatures.

Psalm 139.13 tells us that God knows about and values each pregnancy from the point of conception. However, not only is each human life valuable, it also *has a purpose* (see Psalm 139.15, 16). In other words, the person writing the psalm imagines that all his life ('all the days that were formed for me') was written in God's 'book' even before it 'existed'.

The Old Testament also contains the earliest teaching against killing. In the Ten Commandments, God forbids the taking of life (see Exodus 20.13). It is argued that abortion counts as 'killing', on the assumption that the foetus is a person. However, the law does not treat the foetus as a person.

Even so, a very early Christian writing called the *Didache* (written *c.* AD 70, and therefore contemporary with many New Testament writings) states explicitly that abortion is wrong.

Contemporary Christian teaching

These ideas still dominate Christian thinking. Here are some examples.

- 'Life must be protected with the utmost care from the moment of conception: abortion and infanticide [killing newborns] are abominable crimes': **Second Vatican Council**, 1962–5.
- 'Human life is sacred. All men must recognize this fact': Pope Paul VI, *Humanae Vitae*, 1968. (This encyclical (see the glossary on page 19) contained important teaching and included a ban on artificial contraception.)
- 'Every person sincerely open to truth and goodness can . . . come to recognize . . . the sacred value of human life from its very beginning until its end': Pope John Paul II, *Evangelium Vitae*, section 2, 1995 (see page 26).

While the Church of England also teaches a high respect for life, it does not take such an absolute view. So, when discussing the value of the unborn child, an Anglican report called *Personal Origins* states: 'the foetus is to be specially respected and protected' (Board for Social Responsibility, 1985). Although the report goes on to condemn abortion as a form of contraception, it says 'the life of the mother is regarded as taking precedence over the life of the foetus if there is a conflict'. In other words, the life of the mother is considered more important (more sacred) than that of the foetus.

SUMMARY

1 Moral decisions involve distinguishing between right and wrong. Parents, siblings, teachers and peer groups have a continual effect on shaping what we regard as right and wrong.

2 By our teenage years, we will have made others' attitudes and judgements our own. We will have internalized them and developed our conscience.

3 However, conscience is more than others' attitudes and judgements internalized. Conscience includes the use of our reason to scrutinize our moral decisions: we can choose to behave contrary to the attitudes and judgements that we have internalized.

4 We can scrutinize our choices in a number of ways but three categories – egoism, utilitarianism and deontological choices – help us begin to understand how we tend to make moral choices.

5 Egoism means putting one's own interests first in making moral decisions. What is right is what most benefits oneself.

6 However, it is not always easy to tell whether someone is behaving egotistically. If you act simply egotistically – ignoring the interests of others – they will not cooperate. Therefore, egoists have to take account of others' interests (altruism) so as to get the best outcome for themselves.

7 One form of altruism is making decisions that will benefit the greatest number of people. This ethical choice is illustrated by the way the emergency services apply triage at a disaster scene.

8 This form of altruism can be categorized as utilitarianism, seeking the greatest good for the greatest number.

9 Another approach to making moral decisions is deontological: acting according to what you consider to be your duty. For example, some Christians believe that they have a duty to obey what the Bible teaches or, if they are Roman Catholics, what the Pope teaches (the magisterium). Other Christians tend to regard what their leaders teach as guidance rather than authority.

GOING DEEPER

10 There are three major Christian traditions: Orthodox, Roman Catholic (a denomination in itself) and Protestant. Within the Orthodox and Protestant traditions there are many separate churches and denominations.

11 Each denomination has distinctive teaching, summaries of which can be found on their websites.

12 There is a great deal of overlap between denominations, e.g. all Christians are opposed to killing people. There are also significant differences, e.g. over whether remarriage is permissible.

13 The basis of authority varies according to denomination, e.g. Roman Catholics appeal to the magisterium whereas Protestants appeal to Scripture.

14 There is also variety within denominations: e.g. the magisterium forbids artificial birth control but some Catholics ignore this teaching; and within the Church of England – with its mixed Catholic and Protestant history – conservative Evangelicals might interpret the Bible literally, whereas liberal Anglicans are likely to be more flexible in their interpretation, taking account of a text's historical context.

15 Differences *within* denominations – broadly between 'liberals' and 'conservatives' – can be as significant as differences *between* denominations.

16 'Sanctity of life' denotes the belief that life is precious and of the highest value. Its roots are to be found in the Old and New Testaments.

17 Contemporary Christian teaching about the sanctity of life varies, as the issue of abortion illustrates: for Roman Catholics abortion is an abominable crime, whereas the Church of England takes a less absolute view. For example, Anglicans teach that the life of the mother takes precedence over the foetus' life if there is a conflict.

REVISION QUESTIONS

1 Give three examples of moral decisions.

2 Who provides the earliest influences for shaping our ability to distinguish right and wrong?

3 What is conscience?

4 What is altruism? Give one example.

5 What is egoism? Give one example.

6 What is utilitarianism? Given an example of the application of utilitarian principles.

7 What is the technical term for ethical approaches that are based on duty and obligation?

8 What is the technical name for the sacred teaching authority in the Roman Catholic Church? Who exercises this authority?

GOING DEEPER

9 How do conservative Evangelicals and liberal Anglicans differ in their approach to the authority of the Bible?

10 What is meant by the term 'sanctity of life'?

11 Where do Christians derive their belief in sanctity of life from?

12 What differences are there between Roman Catholic and Anglican teaching about sanctity of life when considering whether abortion is ever permissible?

SOURCES AND ACKNOWLEDGEMENTS

Extracts from the Bible

Unless otherwise noted, biblical quotations are taken from the New Revised Standard Version of the Bible, Anglicized Edition, copyright © 1989, 1995 by the Division of Christian Education of the National Council of the Churches of Christ in the USA. Used by permission. All rights reserved.

Scriptures marked GNB are quoted from the Good News Bible, published by The Bible Societies/HarperCollins Publishers Ltd UK and are copyright © American Bible Society, 1966, 1971, 1976, 1992, 1994.

Extracts marked NJB are taken from The New Jerusalem Bible, published and copyright © 1985 by Darton, Longman & Todd Ltd and Doubleday & Co., Inc., a division of Random House, Inc., and are used by permission.

Extract from liturgy

p. 46, Extract from the Anglican marriage service, *Common Worship: Pastoral Services*, p. 123, copyright © The Archbishops' Council 2000, 2005. <copyright@c-of-e.org.uk>

Other extracts

Other quotations are from the following sources:

p. 15, Albert Schweitzer, *The Philosophy of Civilization*, ch. 26, trans. C. T. Campion (Buffalo, NY: Prometheus, 1987).

p. 21, Church of England briefing paper for bishops, 'Genetics – a background', p. 6(a) (2002); available at www.churchofengland.org/media/45697/genetics.pdf.

pp. 27 and 141, John Paul II, *Evangelium Vitae* (London: Catholic Truth Society, 1995).

pp. 33 and 65, Paul VI, *Declaration on Religious Freedom (Dignitatis Humanae) on the Right of the Person and of Communities to Social and Civil Freedom in Matters Religious* (1965); available at www.vatican.va/archive/hist_councils/ii_vatican_council/documents/vat-ii_decl_19651207_dignitatis-humanae_en.html.

pp. 21, 32, 33 and 136, *Catechism of the Roman Catholic Church* (1993), copyright © Libreria Editrice Vaticana, Citta del Vaticano 1993; available at www.vatican.va/archive/ENG0015/_INDEX.HTM#fonte.

p. 34, Ann Furedi, 'Abortion matters', *Living Marxism*, 12 November 1999.

p. 35, 'Illuminata', the Clergy for Choice newsletter (Washington, DC: The Religious Coalition for Reproductive Choice, 2000).

p. 39, John Paul II, from Karol Wojtyla (John Paul II), *The Anthropological Vision of Humanae Vitae*, trans. William E. May, available at www.christendom-awake.org/pages/may/anthropvisionjpii.htm; and from the General Audience of Wednesday, 8 August 1984, section 2, available at www.ewtn.com/library/papaldoc/jp2tb117.htm.

p. 40, Church of England Board for Social Responsibility (1980), from 'Abortion: a briefing paper', prepared by the General Synod's Mission and Public Affairs Division in 2005; available at www.churchofengland.org/media/45673/abortion.pdf.

p. 40, Church of Scotland Board of Social Responsibility, *Abortion in Debate* (Edinburgh: Quorum Press, 1987).

p. 41, Gordon Linney, quoted in the *Irish Times*, 13 March 2002.

p. 48, 'The family', Article XVIII in *The Baptist Faith and Message* (2000); available at http://shakinandshinin.org/TheBaptistFaithAndMessage2000PlusCommentary.pdf.

p. 65, Paul VI, *Declaration on the Relation of the Church to Non-Christian Religions* (Nostra Aetate) (1965); available at www.vatican/archive/hist_councils/ii_vatican_council/documents/va-ii_decl_19651028_nostra_aetate_en.html.

p. 77, John XXIII, *Pacem in Terris*, sections 126–7 (1963; London: Catholic Truth Society, 2002).

pp. 77–8, House of Bishops, *Evaluating the Threat of Military Action against Iraq: A contribution to the debate by The House of Bishops*, 9 October 2002; available at www.casi.org.uk/info/churcheng/020320coewar.pdf.

p. 89, Andrew Mitchell, 'How a little loan goes a long way', *The Times*, 1 September 2006.

p. 100, United States Conference of Catholic Bishops, 'A statement of the Catholic Bishops of the United States', issued 15 November 2000; available at www.usccb.org/sdwp/criminal.shtml#introduction.

p. 108, Paul VI, *Justice in the World* (1971), quoted from paragraph 8 of the English translation on the website of the Office for Social Justice, St Paul, Minnesota, www.osjspm.org/majordoc_justicia_in_mundo_offical_test.aspx.

p. 108, John Paul II, 'The ecological crisis: a common responsibility', the Pope's World Day of Peace message, 1 January 1990.

p. 141, Paul VI, *The Regulation of Birth: Encyclical letter of Pope Paul VI* (Humanae Vitae) (London: Catholic Truth Society, 1968).

p. 141, Church of England Board for Social Responsibility, *Personal Origins: Report of a working party on human fertilization and embryology of the Board for Social Responsibility* (London: Church House Publishing, 1985; updated 1996).

Picture credits

The publisher would like to thank the following for permission to use photographs and illustrations:

Anglican Communion Office/Jim Rosenthal, p. 90; Cynthia Black, p. 63; Christian Aid/Brenda Hayward, p. 109; Christian Aid/Antoinette Powell, p. 85; Sophie Dean, pp. 26, 125; Dein Freund der Baum, p. 130; Lord Habgood, p. 27; Howard League for Penal Reform, p. 99; Jubilee Centre/Faraday Institute, p. 105; Andrew Linzey, p. 15; Dan McCurry, pp. 10, 60; Press Association, pp. 9, 13, 14, 19, 29, 34, 36, 37, 38, 57, 59, 60, 61, 62, 64, 68, 69, 70, 71, 78, 126, 139; Sheldon Press, p. 138; Shutterstock, pp. 11, 12, 18, 20, 31, 49, 56, 59, 73, 75, 94, 96, 99, 104, 106, 110, 112, 113, 114, 118, 119, 123, 131; Richard Smith, pp. 83, 84, 97, 98; Steve Wheeler, p. 125.

Every effort has been made to acknowledge fully the sources of material reproduced in this book. The publisher apologizes for any omissions that may remain and, if notified, will ensure that full acknowledgements are made in a subsequent edition.